Manage
Your Plant
for **Profit**
and Your
Promotion

MANAGE
YOUR PLANT
FOR **PROFIT**
AND YOUR
PROMOTION

57389

RICHARD W. OGDEN

amacom
A DIVISION OF AMERICAN MANAGEMENT ASSOCIATIONS

Library of Congress Cataloging in Publication Data

Ogden, Richard W.
  Manage your plant for profit and your promotion.

  1. Industrial management.   2. Factory management.
I. Title
HD31.047   658.2   78-2540
ISBN 0-8144-5466-6

First Printing

To Faye Crider,
the premier plant manager

PREFACE

The person who determines the destiny of any manufacturing facility is the plant manager. No matter what the strengths of the many separate parts, unless the manager welds them into a productive unit there is no continuing success. Top managements are coming to realize this and are putting high quality people into plant manager jobs.

This is as it should be and will have to be. The problem is that despite the basic skills of those selected, the job is so complex that it takes time to learn. And once learned, all that experience must be absorbed.

The genesis of this book was in my own dilemma over what to do in particular situations as a plant manager. I did a lot of looking and talking with other managers and found the same questions and problems recurring, but I found very little published material that could help. So this is a sharing of the real-life experiences common to all plant managers, with the hope it will be related to, learned from, and referred to.

Credit for much of the proven thinking goes to Faye Crider, who spent endless coffee-drinking hours teaching a neophyte engineer; then to Arlene Morris, who carried a new plant manager over the rough places; and to Eddie Will Johnson, Shirley Hardin, and Richard Leonard, who are proving the worth of a good plant manager.

Richard W. Ogden

CONTENTS

YOU'RE THE BOSS

WORKING THROUGH OTHERS

HOME IMPROVEMENTS

YOU'RE THE BOSS

1 | CAPTAIN, CAPTAIN

You're responsible! That's the first, final, inescapable, irreversible fact. Your plant is good or bad because of you. Whatever happens—the successes and the failures—they all come back to you. And that's great! It means the world is yours. Your plant can be anything you want if you make it happen.

And now for the bad part: there's no passing the buck. If some new, young worker does something unbelievably stupid, it's your fault. If one of your most trusted, capable people suddenly goes bananas on the job, it's your fault. There's no way around this basic fact. The plant manager bears the ultimate responsibility.

Lip service won't do. It's easy to nod your head and say, yes, you're responsible, but to see it as a technicality. That won't do. You've got to believe in your heart that anything that goes wrong is your fault.

This is vital. Until you're willing to make this first admission, and accept total responsibility, you're not going to make it. Until you agonize over every little thing that goes wrong and personally feel the weight of the error, you're not ready. Until you make that kind of commitment, you're going to fall short.

That's what makes it so great! If you must bear every

3

responsibility, who but you can claim credit for ultimate success? No one but you. No one.

Sure, there are other people involved. It can never completely be a one-person show. There are too many things to be done, too many details to look after, too many people to be dealt with. There have to be others.

But it's the manager who makes the difference. This is the awesome truth. From the humblest positions to the loftiest, the overall success of the people who occupy them—no matter how talented—depends on the person they work for. That's who ties everything together. That's who supplies the motivation, the means for total accomplishment, the central coordination, who sets the very mood of the plant.

Yes, the very mood of the plant. Have you ever thought about that? It's true. You can tell what kind of manager runs a plant just from being in it. Which, incidentally, is one of the most effective tools you can have to sell yourself when it comes to promotion. The plant itself will do the selling. What more can you ask?

Whether you're working through other people, doing it yourself, or thinking about what needs to be done, the moving force has to be you. If you believe it, the world is your oyster. It's downright exhilarating to know what kind of destiny is in your power. Where others have failed, you can succeed! By your own efforts you achieve what others envy.

You're the captain

It's not unlike a captain and his ship. By definition, his authority, which is ultimate and absolute at sea, dominates the entire crew. You, as manager, are like that with your plant.

There are differences, of course. You can't make anyone walk the plank for plotting mutiny. Your "crew" is not quite so captive or so readily available for work every day. You must go on the principle of persuasion rather than decree. A worker can't be locked in irons for unbecoming conduct. So your approach can't be quite as autocratic, but the effect is the same. *You* supply the leadership. It can't come from your second in command. Nothing can happen without your making it happen.

Staggering, isn't it? That one individual can have so much influence—not only on the work itself, but on the lives of many others. Every single soul in the plant is touched by the abilities of the manager. All that responsibility is great, but can you handle it? There's only one sure way to know and that's to do it. No matter how good you think you are, unless you get things done you're blowing smoke.

It doesn't take much talent to rationalize away problems by saying they're beyond control. There are always excuses that sound so good and are so close to the truth that giving in to them is tempting. Having a few good excuses on hand for the boys up above is good thinking, but when you start believing them, you're in for trouble.

Results

The reason you're promotable (or worth more money) in the first place is because you can do things others can't. If you're stopped for the same reasons they are, why are you better? Because you are you? Well, it doesn't work that way. You'll be judged by results in your plant—results because of you. It all comes back to that.

You must know in your heart that one person can make a difference. You must know without question that that person is the one at the top—you. You must accept the burden that if things are going wrong, or not well enough, it's because you're not doing the job that needs to be done.

This is pretty strong medicine. It's easy to go through the motions, to be satisfied that not everything can go as it should, because some matters are beyond your control.

It's quite another to confront—and conquer—the same trials that have stalled others, to admit the problem is not insoluble but hasn't been corrected yet because you haven't solved it. Yes, sir, that's something else again.

You must have confidence that you are the person to do the job. This confidence must be solid. It must be firmly rooted in the certainty that you can and will do what needs to be done, when it needs to be done. It has to be able to stand the test of the firing line.

It has to be the confidence that you have the job because you are the best one for it. It has to be the confidence that will withstand questioning from others. It has to be the kind of confidence that allows you to make mistakes, admit them, learn from them, and overcome them.

It must be the confidence of leadership. You are the leader, and whatever happens does so because of you. Everyone and everything depends on you. That's the way it is, captain. It's kind of frightening, but if you're going for the ride, what better place than at the helm?

2 ‖ THY WILL BE DONE

Management techniques are good. You know, time planning, management by objectives, X and Y, all that stuff. But do they really get the job done? Does management style make that much difference?

No. The plain, hard fact is that style isn't what matters. Various techniques can help, but that's all.

Sound heretical? Not a bit. What is often forgotten is
that all such techniques and countless more are tools,
pure and simple. They don't take the place of whatever
kind of manager you happen to be; they just help. The
fact remains that bastards and barons are both effective.
Both can run very good producing plants.

Pages and pages could be, and have been, devoted to
what the best style is. You read why one works and one
doesn't when you know better. What you need to understand isn't what's different, but what's the same.

Attitude Does it

How can so many different styles all be effective? The answer is remarkably simple. Attitude. That's
right, attitude. Without question this is the most important quality in a manager. That's a strong statement and
needs emphasis. Unquestionably, the most important
quality in a successful manager is attitude.

Now don't confuse attitude with personality. Or charisma. It has nothing to do with a particular type of
individual, a certain physical specimen, even a management type.

What is attitude? The dictionary defines it as "a state
of mind," and that's close. For the successful manager,
it's a state of mind that the plant will run to potential.
It's an overpowering mental toughness that prevails in
all circumstances. It's a state of mind that keeps a manager going when others have thrown in the towel. It's an
inbred knowledge that what should be done will be
done.

In modern terms it's the power of positive thinking,
the forward movement, the can-do philosophy. And
when you come right down to it there's just the slightest

touch of bullheadedness. It's a mental state that exerts itself when everyone else is down; when problem after problem piles on top of one another; when the last effort has been made and still more is called for; when it's humanly possible but seems impossible. That's when attitude comes through, time and time again.

Attitude is visible in times other than crisis. It's less dramatic in ordinary circumstances, but it's nonetheless present. In fact, every day is where it's most important. Day after day of doing the routine, of establishing the proper method of operation and maintaining it—that's when the groundwork for rising to the occasion is laid.

This management attitude means persistence. When it comes to improving quality, increasing production, or making changes, persistence is what counts.

It's not a Pollyanna attitude. That's counterproductive. Many dreamers have failed because they weren't realistic enough to understand the situation. This attitude is based on a hard realism that few can share.

At the same time there is a trace of Pollyanna. The edge that keeps the manager up when subordinates are down. The touch that allows the manager to see the situation as temporary and continue on an up keel. Down days for such a manager aren't impossible, but they're very rare. Even then, they're a brief luxury.

This attitude maintains enthusiasm above and beyond that of others. It keeps the manager the example, and that's quite all right. It's the mental quality of the manager who is looked to for guidance, who should be looked to for guidance, and who knows how to get enough fire extinguishers when Rome is about to burn.

This attitude keeps the manager searching for various techniques, then rejecting or using or developing parallel ones. It means constant vigilance for whatever is needed to get the job done. It's an overriding mental capacity that carries others with you, bringing the whole as you go.

This is the attitude you must have. It's one that will not allow you to falter in the pursuit of your goals.

3 | THAT FIRST STEP

Nothing just happens. Great plans are fine, but unless you're in control and everyone acknowledges that control, you're whistling Dixie. So establishing your command is a basic step as manager.

Sound simple? You're the boss so it should be automatic. You give the order and it's done. You call the tune and the dancers dance. What could be simpler? Nothing. Nothing at all if you want only lip service from your people.

After all, why should they listen to you? If you're new or have been second in command, you're a freshman as far as your workers know. Before you earn their confidence and loyalty, you have to show them you're the leader. To do that, you have to be decisive immediately, yet you must be careful not to make changes without thinking them through. That's the tricky part. How do you do both? How do you make that move that establishes your control but doesn't upset the apple cart?

It isn't easy, but it's not impossible. You don't have to do anything earth-shattering. Not right away, at least. You just have to make your presence known.

High visibility

Begin by making yourself visible. Get out and be seen, in all kinds of places. Don't get caught in the routine of just hitting the high spots. Let everybody see you. Circulate through the plant. Visit if you like, frown if you must, smile if you can, but above all let as many as possible see you as much as possible.

In the course of your visits ask questions. Who are those people? What are they doing? Is that standard procedure? What happens before? What happens next? What's the name? Been here long? Tell me about your job.

You're never sure what kind of situation you're walking into, but few people can resist personal or professional questioning. Remember, you're not trying to win a popularity contest. You're letting people know you're there and that you have a right to be wherever you please in the plant. You're establishing yourself, and that's a point you should never lose sight of. For the plant manager, high visibility always pays dividends.

Next, look for something that obviously needs to be changed. Housecleaning is a good start. Unless the manager you replaced was superhuman, there's going to be housekeeping that can be improved. The results of your efforts will be visible to all. The more you find, the better. Assign the different cleanup areas to different supervisors. It will tell you a world about them.

It will get people used to doing what you tell them and let everyone see that you're directing activities. But be prepared for unexpected resistance. It may seem obvious, but your first test will come in this mundane chore. That's good; it gives you a chance to see and learn from the start.

By the way, don't prejudge the supervisors who need to improve housekeeping the most. All of us develop bad habits, and routine tends to blind us to them. You'll get some bias, sure, but don't close the book.

Another area you can attack early is procedures. Often people do things just because that's the way they've always been done. Find a procedure to simplify or change. People will get the idea.

Another good early move is holding meetings. Just make sure those who attend are carefully selected, a solid agenda is prepared, and you are in control. Or you can do the reverse and eliminate meetings you see no purpose in. Or hold them less often, or change the format. Do what you must to put your stamp on them.

Don't get cornered

While establishing yourself, avoid no-escape showdowns. You can't run and hide if there's nowhere to go. So try to structure all situations to avoid a confrontation. You need time to prepare to fight! You need to know as much about the battleground as possible. You need to initiate whenever possible. You don't want to open too many wounds until you are ready.

That's why it's better to make your early moves as innocuous as possible. Even when you're right as rain there will be some resentment. So don't make it any worse than it has to be. When you're more solidly established you might want to attack head on, but wait until you can do it on your terms.

Naturally the time will come, all too soon, when you must go to the trenches, when you must make decisions you're not adequately prepared to make—and don't want to make. But there's no choice. So get all the counsel you can, all the available expertise. Then make the decision and let everyone know, right or wrong, it was yours.

When you can, however, lay the groundwork first. Make your presence known without ruffling too many feathers. Not so surprisingly, many of your early antagonists will turn into your staunchest allies. So don't be too quick out of the starting blocks. Just be quick enough that your people know you not only are in the race but are going to win.

4 | YOUR TEAM

Day one. That's when you start building the team that's going to get you promoted. From initial contact, you should be finding, building, training, developing, and leading this very special group. Yes, very special. Because without them you're dead, you're zero, and you'd better remember it. In the end, it's this group that will make or break you.

Be realistic. No manager can be on the spot whenever a decision has to be made. There are simply too many details to cover day in and day out. You need help! And the kind you have is entirely up to you.

Building a plant team is different from building a corporate one. To start with, you don't have the option of tracking down better people through expensive headhunters. You've got to go with what's there. On the surface, this can be a pretty grim proposition.

But it's not that bad. Somebody's doing something right or there wouldn't be a plant at all. They may not be doing as well as they should, they may not look like the cream of the crop, but the talent's there someplace. It always is. It's what you do with this raw material that will make the difference.

So find the talent and put it to good use. There's nothing automatic about the process. It takes a lot of looking, talking, and observing. It takes a lot of time too. There are going to be false starts. Many candidates who seem impressive at first will pale with the test of time. Many will be reluctant to show their colors for various reasons. That doesn't mean they're not there; it just means the search will take a little longer.

Find the doers

What are you looking for? In a nutshell, people who can get the job done. Find those who want to do it, give them the support and opportunity, and they're yours.

That may sound simple, but it's not. The easy part is getting people to work hard and perform beyond past efforts. That's what they want too. The hard part is gaining their loyalty so that real progress can be made. Yes, personal loyalty to you is essential. You're going to take your people above and beyond, so you need their absolute faith.

Your goal is to make these key people an extension of yourself. Think about it—an extension of yourself through others! The best part is that it will be to their benefit as well as yours. Your thoughts, your dreams, your dedication will find life through these lieutenants. Your programs will become as vital to them as they are to you.

And they'll love it! It will give them a chance to grow on their own, to develop their own thinking. An opportunity they didn't realize they wanted has a chance for life.

One caution. Everyone in a trusted position won't become one of your lieutenants. Many will still do their jobs, probably better because of you, but will never really be your people. True trusted lieutenants are rare. So you need to develop the others too. Develop them to the fullest, support them, give them opportunity. But know the difference between those who are led and those who are truly with you.

In your search, look for those people who are always at the hub of an activity. Whether they have direct responsibility or not, they get the job done. Your objective is to find these strong, loyal team members who will help you build the kind of plant you want. Avoid hangers-on and flatterers. You want producers!

And there's no faking. To get loyal and productive people, you have to have something yourself. So it's dangerous. Can you afford close scrutiny?

Yes, certainly! People don't expect perfection. They do expect strong leadership and support—and your expectation of perfection from them. Because they want to do well. That's one of the qualities that attracted you to them. So you have an obligation to expect a lot.

These people will probably take up what seems an inordinate amount of your time, especially during the early stages. That's necessary. The only way you can cultivate and develop them properly is by spending time with them.

The drawback is that other people might resent or misinterpret your actions. If you are a male and she's the other, or if you're a female and he's the other, you're open to whispers. It's a risk you have to take. You must work with the talent wherever it lies. Just make sure that's all that develops.

With time must come patience. You must expect a lot, even demand it, but be realistic. It's a long-term proposition. There are going to be mistakes, disappointments, frustrations, and soul searchings. You're going to wonder. Other people are going to make you wonder. That's natural, normal.

But stick to your guns! In the building process mistakes are inevitable. You're striving to get your people to reach a certain level. They're not as good as you yet. Maybe they never will be. But through your support they're going to be much stronger.

Protect, then wean

With support must come protection. As your people learn and make mistakes, you don't want them hurt too badly. They're going to be down and you're going to buck them up. There are going to be times when discouragement sets in. You'll have to carry them over some pretty rocky terrain. That's normal. It happens to the best. Everyone has doubts and gets discouraged.

But then comes a time of weaning. Too much support is self-defeating. A crisis will come when you must turn your back and let them sink or swim. If you've been right, they'll swim. If you haven't, they'll sink. You had your money on the wrong horse.

After the weaning comes true development. Your people will have new confidence to handle their responsibilities and to assume greater responsibilities. That's what you're after—good, solid decision making at the lowest possible level.

You will become more of a consultant than boss. You'll still have to lead, but now you can change direction in your endeavors. Your team will start building teams of its own, with the same basic goal of giving as much responsibility as possible to the lowest possible levels. And as your team begins to handle the day-to-day problems, you can turn your energies to the quantum jump.

The big plus

Another dividend is that as your team gets stronger, so will you. There's no choice. You can't afford to let your people down. As they do more, they're going to know more and expect more from you. Eventually your standards are going to become their standards. If you're tempted to take a short cut, you won't be able to. How would it look? What would they think?

Your people won't let you be less than you should be. They won't allow you to get down. It's a great system! The better you are, the better they are, and the better you are. They benefit, the plant benefits, and you benefit.

That's why building a team is worth every minute of your precious, patient time.

5 | STAND, LOOK, LISTEN

You've got to know what's going on. No matter what kind of leader you are, no matter how many good ideas you've got salted away, no matter what your potential, unless you know what's happening, you're not going to do much.

That's a fact of life. Before you can improve or innovate you've got to know what the current situation is. Granted it's not too hard to go in and make a lot of quick changes and impress everybody that you're the boss. But what's the purpose? There's nothing to making changes. Many won't hurt anything, some will do some damage, and a few, the right few, will make things better. Those are the ones you're after.

Whether you're new on the job or have been there a while, there will be improvements to be made. How do you decide what those are? Just get out and find out. The method is simple: stand, look, listen.

Where to stand

Where to stand's no problem. Certain areas in the plant are naturals. The places where you can see several things going on at one time. They're one-shot views of critical areas. They're places where you are accessible to people going by. Or the places that give you an overview of the whole plant.

What do you do after you've found these places? Nothing but look and listen. And learn. Learn what's going on. Learn who's doing what. Learn what people are supposed to be doing.

If you can't figure it out, ask! But wait a while; there's no reason to advertise your temporary ignorance. Besides, if you wait just a bit, understanding will come, and it will increase with time.

That doesn't mean you shouldn't ask questions. If there's something especially puzzling, it's better to ask and find out than wonder. Questions are also great tools for giving directions. If you phrase one that prompts a subordinate to remedy a situation, you've accomplished something. If you use one that teaches a subordinate, you've achieved a great deal.

Don't worry about making people nervous by standing around. They may think it's a strange custom, but they'll get used to it. In fact, when you get down to the hub of things, workers would rather have the boss out among them than hiding in the office.

The next step is making yourself accessible. Let people know they can get to you, talk to you, communicate with you. The people doing the work provide the genesis of a great many ideas. But you must hear what they are saying. That's a little different from listening.

You know what it's like. It's happened to you. The listener smiles and nods in agreement, but everything goes in one ear and out the other. It turns the speaker off. Sure, you're going to hear plenty that should be turned off, but you're also going to hear things you really need to know.

The challenge is to listen, really listen, to what your people have to say. If you don't, they're going to stop talking. They're not dumb. They can tell if you're really interested or just going through the motions. You'll shut them off. And in the process you'll be hurting yourself.

To take the plant to the heights you envision, you've got to get as much information about the operation as possible. You won't get it if you turn your people off. Keep them talking to you!

No gossip

A word of caution here. You don't want gossip. You don't want people talking about others personally or digging up dirt. You don't want your supervisors to think you're going behind their backs. You've got to allay suspicions that you're out to get somebody or something on somebody.

Just be open and the same with everyone. Don't encourage personal comments. Don't worry, there'll be plenty of legitimate information coming your way.

With this information you'll get a feel for your operation—not just for the people themselves but for the system. You'll become attuned to the movement of the plant, as it is, as it should be. After a while you'll be able to tell what kind of day you're having just by walking through the plant.

Your empathy will be so great that when you're gone and come back, you won't feel right. You'll be out of tune. On the surface you still know what's going on, but you won't have the pulse of what's happening. Until you get that feeling, until you have a basic communion with your plant, you can never take it to the greatness that it deserves.

So get out there and stand around. Find out what's happening, listen to what's happening, and finally become the focal point of what's happening.

The factory floor is a great place to think. Go after ideas from others as well as your own. Let the enthusiasm you've generated in others renew your own when it falters. All things will come if you are a part of what's going on. And the only way to know, to do, to keep current, is to be there.

6 ‖ LET THEM KNOW

Communication is kind of like the weather. Everybody talks about it, but you have to wonder if anyone does anything about it.

So many times corporate leaders cite communication problems as their biggest bugaboo. If only they had better communication profits would soar!

Overdramatic? Not really. That's why you hear so much about it. That's why the concept is overworked and the word overused. Communication can make the difference between success and failure. Without it, very little can be accomplished. Used properly, it can help you leap mountains with a single bound.

Communication is vital in every phase of your operation. Your people have to know what's going on and what's expected of them if they're ever going to do what you want.

Robert Townsend, in his book *Up the Organization,* was so heretical as to suggest there should be *no* secrets in an organization because secrets are a great impediment to communication. But there has to be some secrecy, simply because rumors abound so vigorously. You already know how even the most innocent comment can give rise to the wildest tales.

An excellent way to combat rumors is to get your people in the habit of expecting you to tell them what's going on. Convince them that the facts will be forthcoming, and from the proper source.

Employee contact

And be open with everyone. Have your conversations and dealings out where no one can accuse you of skulking around. That doesn't mean you should never share a confidence with an employee. But make sure what is said is the secret, not the fact that you talked with someone.

One of the greatest communication devices available is having your office right on the production floor. Now it's nice to envision a big office away from the crowd, with plush carpets and upholstered furniture, where visitors can be impressed. But if you run your plant right, and that kind of thing appeals to you, it can come later. Your mission at present is to run the plant in the best possible way. To do that you have to be out where the action is.

So get your office next to or in the middle of things. Make it as open as possible. Use as many windows as space and construction permit. Don't worry about people thinking you're spying on them; you're going to be watched a lot more than you're going to watch. Then encourage all your people to stop by. Let them know you're available.

Start by arriving a good half-hour before the daily operation begins. Circulate in the plant, but stick close to home base so you can be found if anyone wants you. Stay during lunch times on occasion. Do it sporadically or on certain days if you like. Just make sure people know that you're there and available.

Don't make any secret of who comes to see you. There'll be a lot less commotion that way. Encourage conversation by making everyone feel important enough to talk to. Make sure all your people know they are included in the tacit invitation to enter. Convey the idea that your time is not so valuable that you can't share a minute with them, whoever they are.

Of course, at first some people will monopolize you, but this will pass. Don't worry about it and be as courteous to these people as you are to everyone else.

Tell it like it is

Once you've got employees talking to you and asking questions, you must respond properly if you want the relationship to develop. People will be turned off in a hurry if they feel your openness is a façade.

When people ask you questions, answer them. Tell them what they want to know, if you know. If you can't say, tell them that too. They'd much rather hear that than feel you lied to them.

If you don't know, freely admit it. You're not expected to have all information well documented in your head. You'll gain a lot more respect that way than by trying to bluff your way through. If you can get the answer, tell them. Then do it and get back to whoever asked. If you can't find out, let them know that too. Everyone who asks a question has the right—yes, the right—to an answer.

But be careful of partial answers or answers that imply something you did not intend. Beware of answers that let the questioner draw conclusions or of answers you think people want to hear.

Remember the "telephone game"? One person whispers something to the next person, and so on around the circle, until the last person states what was heard out loud. Invariably, the last person has heard something quite different from the original.

Add this natural distortion to everyone's predilection

to exaggerate and it's no wonder the wildest, most re-markable rumors abound. People are going to make up things just for devilment, and if you give them the smallest leeway, they'll run wild.

Sometimes an employee will pump you for informa-tion prematurely and it will be impossible to lie. When this happens, make sure supervisors and others who should know are informed immediately. You don't like to be surprised by information that you should have, and neither do your supervisors. They shouldn't be! It's not fair to them and in many instances will hurt you.

Similarly, if an employee raises a question about the work or job, let the immediate supervisor know. Super-visors need to be informed. Just make sure they under-stand that even though you want direct communication with your people, nothing is going on behind their backs.

If it's news

It's obvious that you should inform your peo-ple of anything dramatically new. What's tough is re-membering what is new. Many times you become so familiar with developments as they occur that you for-get others are unaware of them. So keep alert to what is new and needs telling.

You must also determine who should know first. News should come from the top down. Even in mass announcements, it's wise to give your supervisors a preview of what is going to be said. If you establish a procedure or checklist and follow it, special announce-ments should be no problem.

Deciding on the day-to-day information that should be disseminated is more difficult. How do you formally announce the routine matters that you take for granted? How do you sift out items of general interest

that are worth repeating? How can you get your job
done if you spend all day trying to decide what to tell
everybody you're doing when you're not doing it because you're too busy telling?

Techniques

It's not as complicated as it sounds. Start by
holding regular meetings with your supervisors. Set up
a time that's convenient to all—during morning breaks,
at lunch once a week, or right after work every day
several days a week. Keep these meetings short and informal. Refer to notes you've made during the day.
Have the supervisors comment on their section, on what
you've said, and on any questions their people have
raised.

Encourage open communication between supervisors
and their subordinates. Let the word get out that supervisors are interested in employees' questions, that they
feed them to you, and that information will get back to
the people. The system is nothing more than word of
mouth. It will take some time to establish it, and there's
sure to be some distortion. But if enough people get the
right information, and others know they can get clarification when wanted, it will work well.

An added dividend, when you get your supervisors
together regularly, is that you teach and develop them
on the sly. You also give supervisors a feeling of involvement, another necessary part of your long-term plan.

If your plant has a PA system, use it for special messages. Some managers take to this and some don't. If
your machines are running as they should and you'd
have to break into work to get the point across, there are
better ways. But for a big announcement it can be
effective.

Bulletin boards are a tried and true method. Don't

underestimate them. Just be sure to separate announcement boards from those for private messages or official laws, or your words will get lost in the shuffle. People look at bulletin boards! They read what's on them. Of course, you'll have to prepare your messages in advance, but they don't have to be anything fancy. Handwritten notes will do.

You might also use a blackboard for short messages or information that changes daily, such as production results, quality results, greetings, or inspirational thoughts. Put the blackboard where people can see it as they enter or leave.

You can call meetings with your employees on a regular basis (weekly, monthly, quarterly). Get a different group of workers in each time. Chat with them on things you know that they don't. Ask them to respond, question, or comment. Keep it loose. If you handle it right, you'll get some great returns.

Occasionally you might want to have a big meeting. Invite the whole plant if possible, or large blocks of workers. This meeting should be structured with a fixed agenda. You can use it to make a particularly important announcement or as a kick-off meeting followed by smaller group sessions.

Another effective means of communication is a newsletter. Don't start frowning. It doesn't have to be fancy and it's really not that tough. You can do it with a typewriter and mimeograph, or even get one printed at minimal cost. It's not the appearance that counts so much as the idea that you want people informed.

Read through a few newsletters for some standard topics. Keep a log of past or upcoming events. Include all the personal data you have room for. Get feedback from supervisors and workers on what they would like to have included.

Employees are more interested in the plant than you

think. They want to know about customers, product acceptance, business prospects, company officials. They like to know what the company is doing, what the styles are going to be. They're even interested in any problems the company faces, and may come to your rescue on occasion. If the problem's serious they'll know sooner or later, so level with them and maybe they can help.

Workers need to know

People need to be informed if they are to give the performance you're after. This is the very cornerstone of productivity.

In this day and time no one escapes the ravages of change. It's a fact of modern manufacturing. Your people are going to be called upon for flexibility never before imagined. The surprising thing is they will respond if they know what's going on. If they're used to being told what's happening—the pros and cons of a decision, the necessity of a change—they will much more readily go along.

By and large workers today are more educated and less disciplined than their predecessors. They are unaccustomed to authority and used to questioning everything. You can be stiffnecked and say it isn't right, but it won't do any good. You're going to have to go with what you've got.

It's not all negative. If they can think, they can understand. Just because a value is questioned doesn't mean the value won't be accepted. It's going to take a little longer to get the workers of today to be producers, but they will be. They can be made to be. Often they don't mind the work nearly as much as they mind not knowing the why of it. So what's the secret? Communication!

And you're the one who's responsible for seeing they

get the word. It's a tall order, because there is no way to cover everything you should. Something's going to get left out. Sad as it may be, sometimes somebody's not going to get the word. That's why it's so important to be conscious of the need for people to know and to make sure that as many people as possible are as fully informed as possible.

Ask yourself every day, "What do I know that they should?" And when you get an answer, tell them!

7 | BLAME THE SYSTEM

It's an admirable trait to stand up and accept responsibility when something unpopular has to be done. No one can help but admire the person who is ready to take the blame for every action.

After all, you should be a person of conviction. Right is right and that's it, right?

Wrong. Right is what has to be, no question about it. But right is wrong if it makes you the heavy unnecessarily. You're not in a popularity contest, but you need as many people on your side as possible. So when something comes along that your people are going to find hard to digest, don't take it on the chin just to prove your toughness.

Remember, your goal is to be the perfect manager, not the perfect martyr. To be that perfect manager, you're going to have to do things, or cause things to be done, that are highly unpopular with your employees. You know they have to be done. There is no question in your mind. But you also know it will be in the face of hostility.

That hostility can be caused by any number of things. It may be a policy change. You understand the reasons but your people do not and therefore become miffed. Or it could be a personnel change. Someone everybody likes needs to be replaced or dropped, but doesn't want to be replaced or dropped, and nobody else wants you to do it. You can bet on having that to contend with.

Or it might be a routine work change, like staggering lunch hours. Because of conditions you know it has to be done, but people don't like it one bit. The list goes on. You'll be faced with doing many things that you don't totally support and that you know will be unpopular. You expect heavy resistance. But you have no choice.

Don't be the heavy

What do you do? Easy. Blame the system. If there's got to be a bastard in the move, make sure it's not you. Remember, you've got to live with and mold your people. The system is cold and impersonal and doesn't have to live with anybody. Everybody's got to accept it— with you as protector, naturally.

You say that's not fair. You're the company's representative, hand-chosen by the hierarchy to be the person on the spot. So if the company makes an unpopular change, you've got to stand up and say "I'm the company representative, so I'm responsible."

Poppycock! One of the best reasons to have a system is to have something impersonal to blame.

If you have to personalize it, blame it on the boss. That's one thing higher-ups are good for. Your boss is at least one step away, probably physically removed, and can afford to be the heavy.

Many times your people will accept something they don't like if they think they have your sympathy. They can't have that and blame you too. So lay the fault where it'll do the most good. Blame your boss. Be the good guy. Just make sure the job gets done.

Don't feel you're doing the boss dirty, unless you really are. You don't have to shout about an ignorant ogre bent on destroying the working class. That's not called for. Sympathize by saying you know it's going to be tough, but you have to go along because the boss has given you no choice.

If you don't want to make it personal, blame the "head office" or something nebulous. Do whatever makes you most comfortable and allows you to get it done without arousing antagonism. You're not a shirking coward. You're doing the sensible thing!

Rules too

Another great tool for the dynamic manager are the "rules." They are often better to blame than the boss. When you decide something unpopular has to be done use the convenient crutch: "It's the rules." Sometimes it's the easiest, least painful method of getting your way.

Your conscience may be hammering now. You think it's not fair and even smacks of being underhanded. It isn't so.

As you start to move the plant, to bring it into line with corporate thinking, you'll often be moving for reasons beyond the understanding of your people. You know understanding will come with time, but any explanation now would fall on deaf ears. In short, you'll have to do things only you have knowledge of, and you can't afford to lose your people in the process.

There's another good reason for blaming the rules. If you use the rules, and everyone is bound by the same ones, you have reached the ultimate in fairness. At times this may be hard to believe. On the surface that one exception will do so much good and so little harm. Why should your good and faithful people be dealt with like the bad ones? What's fair about that?

You're right, as far as it goes. Some people will be hurt. Living by the rules will create apparent discrepancies. That's the way it is.

Managing by exception may seem the way to go, but it's the road to disaster. There's no way in the world you can keep changing your standards and treat everyone equally. There is no fairness when exceptions become the rule. In the long run everybody suffers, and those you wanted to protect usually come out much worse because of your "generosity."

Abide by the rules and everyone is treated alike. They know what to expect. They have a standard to go by. Hard decisions are easier to make—and take—if rules are rules.

Lay the blame elsewhere whenever it will work to your advantage. It's not that you don't have the courage of your convictions or that you're afraid to stand up and be counted. You're doing the politic thing! Many misguided managers have failed to heed this opportunity and have lived with the consequences. Don't let it happen to you.

Do blame the system. Do use your boss to advantage. Do rely on the rules for support. In the long run you'll be better off for it.

8 | A LITTLE FEAR

You agree that the days of the unfeeling, insensitive strong-armed boss are gone. In your management efforts, you want to be liked.

It's better that way. You motivate your people and they do the job because they want to. Your only whip is leadership, which you wield with a deft and soft touch. There's no more badgering people. In fact, you get results through your quiet efforts and example. There's no reason to push too hard. You don't like to and the people don't need it.

But what about being too nice? That's right, you don't want to be too nice or that will hurt you too.

It's sad but true. Most people need a touch of fear to perform up to their potential. They must be a little bit afraid of the boss's wrath. It's this fear, this knowledge that if they go too far wrong they're going to face severe consequences, that puts the fine edge on your subordinates.

It can be too extreme, of course. That's not only counterproductive but self-defeating. People can't be afraid to turn around because you might say boo. You couldn't perform in that kind of environment and neither can they, although a few do thrive on it.

Your relationships with your subordinates should be built on mutual trust. They must have confidence that you are a reasonable boss and faith in your support of them. But—and it's a big but—they also need to know you can get mad. They should be afraid of doing something that would cause you to become aroused.

The enemy

The great enemy you are fighting is complacency, a threat to us all. Precious few can rise above this creeping, malicious malady. Even the most conscientious and capable will need an occasional push.

Then there's that great ally of complacency, routine. Routine's a killer. It lulls people into losing their sharpness. It gets people used to things. It turns a critical eye into a comfortable one. Instead of finding the wrong, it lives with accepting what is.

Routine breeds terrible offspring. Sloppiness for one. Laziness for another. And bad habits for a third. These are the culprits managers must look out for, not only in their people but also in themselves.

Everybody needs reminding. That's human nature. People need to understand they must remind themselves. As a manager, you have to remind them and train them to be self-reminders. People must know when they're slipping. They need to know they will be held accountable. They need to know that if they stray too far from the proper path they're going to feel the fury of your wrath.

Easy does it

That fury doesn't always have to be withering. You don't have to descend in full anger on all occasions. In fact, you probably shouldn't most of the time. If the infraction is minor or understandable or one you can use to teach with, a simple, easy correction should be enough. Otherwise, you're going to lose your people. They'll turn to shadows, jump on command, and do absolutely nothing for your cause.

Unfortunately, small corrections aren't always enough. Your subordinates will get used to them and not be too concerned if they don't feel the occasional bite. Sure, they don't want to disappoint you and they still want to do the job, but they can get too comfortable. So, there has to be a little fear of giving cause for you to be aroused. People have to know that if they let down too much, it's going to be mighty uncomfortable, at least for a while.

That little touch of fear will keep your people on their toes.

9 ‖ DISPUTES

You're going to be in the middle. There's no way around it. No matter how fine your people or how well you've trained them, you're going to wind up between them.

It'll be worse at the start. Some people are just plain going to test you. They're going to find out what you're made of. They'll poke and probe to see where you're strong and where you're weak. They'll use little tricks to see how gullible you are, if you can be manipulated. Yes, sir, they're going to try.

It won't just be the people close to you. Everyone will want to test you—people in the plant, people in the office, people on the staff. That means you end up in the middle. In the middle of arguments, disagreements, personal feuds, professional jealousies, petty ploys, and occasional genuine misunderstandings.

Remember, you're the ultimate authority. You're the one who can make everything better, the one who can make the hurt go away. So people will want to find out if you are going to take care of their particular hurt.

They'll want to know if you can be taken advantage of, if there's anything you will or won't do to help their cause. You'd best be prepared.

It's not that they're bad. It's not that they're deliberately trying to put something over on you. It's just that people are that way. They see any disagreement, heated or otherwise, from one set of eyes only. They'll always exaggerate the facts so you'll understand their side. Each subordinate wants you as an ally.

It's always slanted

Therefore when you hear any version of an argument, remember it's slanted. Each side tends to appear clean and blameless. This tendency is easy to understand, and easy to prove if you're honest with yourself. Think about a misunderstanding you had with someone else. How did you present your version to a third party? Even if you admitted fault, chances are you painted a picture in your favor.

Keep that in mind. Whether it be your most trusted supervisor, your second in command, or even your boss, the story is always one-sided. And the telling makes you involved. By listening and knowing you've been dragged in. First people do it to test and then because it's natural. Either way you're in. Your judgment will be called for.

Don't go off half-cocked. That's rule number one. It's easy when someone favored gives you a heated version of an argument with someone not so favored. When emotions are running high, there's an urge for quick action and proper chastisement.

Guard against this reaction! You cannot afford to be hasty in your judgment. You must not decide until you get all the facts. Don't chew anyone out or implement some half-thought-out idea without learning as much as you can. There's time. There's always time enough if you'll use it.

Getting the facts

Talk to everyone involved, even a third party if possible. While listening, ask questions. Don't let a monologue overpower you. Make the talker give full details. When dealing with a third party, be circumspect, as long as you find out what you want to know. Question any discrepancies you find.

A word of caution. You are not conducting an inquisition. Don't make it the third degree. If you get the person on the defensive, you're not going to get the facts you need. Be straightforward but not brusque or intimidating.

Don't prejudge people because of personal animosity or past record. Ask the same questions of all. Be persistent until you're satisfied with the results. And be true to your method. Treat all alike, even if you must vary your approach slightly because of circumstances. People will come to appreciate it.

The secret is to be truly fair in all your dealings. Before long even the most contrary will stop working you, most of the time. Others will see that it's pointless to try to take advantage of you.

All in all, you'll pass the test. You won't be so bothered with fabricated or "work you" situations. You'll be able to concentrate on the legitimate differences and misunderstandings, of which there'll still be plenty. Don't worry. Those legitimate disagreements will give you more than enough involvement.

10 | DON'T ASK

A 37-year-old philosopher—who happened to be a plant manager—once said, "If you're not going to like the answer, don't ask the question."

If you think about it, that's pretty good advice. There are questions, and then there are questions. Before you ask one, consider the answer. Often the most innocent question brings a damaging response. So if you don't have to ask a question, and there's a chance you won't like the answer, don't ask.

This is not preaching insurrection. It's no disgrace to ask questions of your boss or someone who's been there before. You're no less a manager, and often you're more of one, if you go to higher authority for a decision.

Sometimes there's no alternative. The decision is beyond your authority and you must go up that ladder. Everyone has gone through that and there's nothing demeaning about it. But there are innumerable situations where it's up to you to make the decision. Day-to-day management is impossible from long distance. Someone on the scene has to be in charge. That's why you're there.

Don't tie your hands

So let's talk about a decision you have to make. You're leaning one way; in fact, you're convinced that's the best way to go. But you hesitate. You don't want to make the commitment, or you want some reassurance. Consequently, you ask your boss. Bam! The answer is to do it the other way, the way you are solidly convinced is wrong.

Now you're hooked. You have no choice. You can beg and plead and argue. But if the boss is adamant, there is nothing you can do. You've forced the boss into giving you a directive.

The freedom you once had is suddenly lost. If you had gone your own way and the decision had worked, it would be very satisfying. If it hadn't worked, chances are you could have caught the error and fixed it, so things would still be fine.

Ask the boss unnecessarily and you change all of that. Once you're told what to do, you've tied your own hands. You've forced someone less qualified than you to make a decision—a decision that could very well come back to haunt you. If it does, there's no one to blame but yourself. By going beyond your requirement for legitimate advice, you've negated your own authority, and you must live with the consequences.

Retain your prerogatives

When you don't need advice, it's imperative to retain your managerial prerogatives. It's impossible to run your plant the way you should or to progress without preserving your independence as a manager. You've got to be free to do and undo. You've got to be willing to take a chance, to trod unchartered ground.

Once you give up your prerogatives in order to protect your hide, you've taken the first step in undermining your own effectiveness. There's no way you can give up authority to an outsider and still exercise dynamic leadership. You've got to be willing to stand by your actions. You cannot keep inviting the boss in for decisions that should be yours and expect to run your own show.

That's not to say you should be secretive about what you're doing. The people you work for should be kept informed. Of course, you may want to give something a little time to jell before you brag; but that's being prudent, not secretive.

In the routine, day-to-day operation, it's your baby. You should feel the burden of responsibility as yours alone. There's no reason every decision should be transmitted up top. Keep the boss posted on general developments, or anything out of the ordinary, but don't bother with your normal routine.

You must also guard against inadvertently getting direction that you neither want nor need. Don't make idle talk by asking what to do. It's better to discuss the weather and anything else neutral than to casually mention something that gets you direction you don't want. Don't ask for specifics, no matter how idly, unless you actually want to be told. Many plans have been nipped in the bud because the subordinate ran out of things to say and turned to things better left unsaid.

Remember, if it's your business, it's your boss's business too. At least bosses regard it as such. And the boss is going to have no compunction about telling you how to go about it if you give the opening.

When it's right and proper, by all means ask for guidance. Take advantage of the knowledge and experience your boss is bound to have. That's what the boss is there for. But if it means getting an answer you don't want and don't need, don't ask.

11 THE GLASS HOUSE

Have you ever wondered what it would be like to live in the proverbial glass house? A dwelling where you were on display for all to see? A place where you fought for a private moment only to find somebody there spying on you?

Wonder no more, my friend, because by becoming a plant manager you've moved into one.

It's hard to believe that any one person could command so much attention. You'd be amazed at how employees take your every action to heart. It's difficult to comprehend how your words are magnified, misconstrued, and twisted. Comments or asides with literally no meaning are repeated and re-repeated as gospel.

This is vital to remember. You're in everybody's eye some of the time and somebody's eye at almost any time. In the plant and out, someone will notice and comment. That's one of the disadvantages of being a manager. People like to know what the boss is doing and they like to talk about it. In many ways a plant is like a small town. People know a lot about other people's business and feel obliged to talk about it. Some of these people are well meaning. You wouldn't believe it from the grief they cause, but they don't mean harm; they're just interested. Unfortunately, that interest can often fan flames that are better left alone. But there's nothing in the world that will keep people from talking.

Those other types

Then there are the people who make unkind and derogatory remarks deliberately. The sad truth is that some people are flat-out troublemakers: They delight in causing problems, and the more they can stir up the better.

Now you can convince yourself that these people wouldn't harm you for the world; you can believe that all their smiles are genuine. Or you can believe that they have hurt someone else, someone you secretly believe deserved it, but would never hurt you intentionally.

Once they are exposed to your charm and charisma, they would never do it to you.

If you believe that, you're kidding yourself. You're doomed to learn the hard way. Sometimes the very people who are the nicest to your face are the ones who stab you in the back the moment it's turned.

There is no new boss who is universally liked. Purging your plant of the viper mouths is a long-term proposition, and it's unlikely you'll ever completely do it. (There are people like that throughout the company too. Don't let them surprise you because you didn't believe such types existed.)

Now those who are deliberately trying to cut you down are definitely a very small group, one that at times many others echo. Their nuisance value is blown out of proportion because they're always agitating. On occasion they can be very annoying and even hurt what you're trying to do. But for the most part these people are no more than a nuisance. Ignore them as best you can.

There'll be times when something so unfair or so unreasonable comes up, and you'll know where from, you'll want to throttle somebody. In a word, don't. If there's no substance to a rumor, it'll go away. You can afford not to pay attention or to be coerced into visibly reacting. Wild talk is certainly not worth reacting to if it's only that.

Don't worry about denying each and every rumor that comes along, no matter how upsetting. That's a sure way of getting more of the same. If people can get to you they surely will keep on trying, so don't let them.

Personal habits

Your only concern should be to make sure your personal and professional habits are above reproach. Be sure that you're not loose with talk and that you perform as you should. For example, you're going to be the first one in the plant each day and the last one to leave. Don't faint. Of course it's early and makes a long day, and you can get tired just thinking about it. But that's the way you have to start.

Getting to work on time is one of the best ways of managing by example. If people see that you don't care enough to be there when things are supposed to be getting cranked up, why should they? Similarly, if you edge out the door before quitting time in the evening, why shouldn't everyone else?

Sure it's tough, but very important. Your people need to see you're there when they come in each morning. They need to know that day in and day out, except for rare occasions, you're going to be with them. That's leadership with reassurance built in. You have to show that you care enough to put in the hours if you expect anyone else to.

What you do during the day is also important. Employees need to see that you're out and around and active. They know if you sit in the office and depend on others for information and getting things done.

You can't lead your people if they don't respect you professionally. They might still like you personally, but if your working day consists primarily of reading magazines in your office, they're going to feel you're not contributing a whole lot. And they're right! Trade journals, you say? Well, they're fine, but not all day, every day.

When you're out and around in the plant you must be aware of what you do and say. It's good to be nice and well liked, but first of all you must be the boss. You're no longer one of the gang. You can't be pompous, but you must guard against kidding or horsing around. That kind of popularity seeking has no place in management.

So who is there for you to associate with in the plant? Precious few, my friend. You cannot appear buddy-

buddy with any individual or group. You certainly can't afford to cozy up to the cute or handsome ones more than others. There is no room for special attention in your job.

Sure, you've got to get out and talk to certain people. In developing your key people, you will spend more time with some than others. But make sure it's on a professional plane. Your workers may not understand that it's professional all the time, but you sure can.

Off the job

How about off the job? Can you be a little more relaxed with your people? Not really, and maybe not as much. In the plant you'll at least have a reason for contact. Outside, socializing with subordinates is almost forbidden. It's a bad practice that you cannot afford.

There is just no way you can retain the proper relationship with subordinates on the job, if you habitually socialize with them off it. Even if you could keep the relationship straight, others would resent it. And rightfully so. Too many objective decisions can have the appearance of favoritism, so why take the chance?

In a way it's too bad because there are many good, solid people in any plant. But you're restricted from cultivating their friendship. For you, the plant is not a spring of social relations. Don't find out the hard way. Many have.

Yes, in many respects the life of a plant manager is a tough row to hoe. You can't be a saint no matter how you're watched. But you can be careful about where you let down the barriers. In the plant, and in the presence of employees, you must always be conscious of what you're doing. You simply can't afford weak moments.

As the boss, you're apart and above. You know you're not any better, and they might suspect as much, but you've got an image to live up to. You are looked up to and at. Yes, you. You're the one who occupies that glass-walled house. And you'd better like it.

12 ∥ FAIR!

You've got to be fair! For the manager, fairness is more important today than ever.

You probably won't argue the need. Chances are you feel that you are fair in your duties. You can probably point to any number of instances where you did exactly what you did, not because you wanted to, but because it was the fair way to go. These undoubtedly confirm in your mind that you treat everyone equally, without favoritism.

In today's plant that's not only a good quality but a necessary one. You face legal consequences that your predecessors never encountered. Fairness is not only an admirable quality but a legislated one. With this in mind, you must be conscious that it is not enough to be fair. You have to go that extra step and be able to prove that you were, are, and will continue to be fair.

This is a warning you must heed! There are documented cases of managers who were burned. These managers not only felt what they did was fair but put in that little extra just to make sure. Then it came home to roost that the rules of fairness had changed. A second or third party injected a different interpretation and all of a sudden the manager faced litigation and penalty.

You must always be conscious of legal fairness. You cannot afford to ignore the fact that you are now accountable to the government for the way in which you manage your plant. So make sure you have a firm and viable reason for all your actions. That reason should stand up not only in your own mind but also in the mind of an outsider—an outsider like the inspector from a federal agency on discrimination.

You're being watched

Many outsiders are looking over your shoulder. Do-gooders are too numerous to count. Everyone has some kind of protector, so don't slight even one insignificant soul. There may be someone waiting in the background to take up or generate a cause.

You may feel it's not that tough to play the legal game. There are many things you can do to give the appearance of fairness. By and large you can fulfill the legal requirements procedurally if not substantively.

But that's self-defeating. You're not really after appearances. You're after what is best for you and your facility. These laws and strictures may be of the nuisance variety, but many were inspired by a real need. It's up to you to surpass that need for the betterment of all. To do so, you must not only act fairly but think fairly.

Does that sound ridiculous? Since you're already doing what is rationally fair, you must already think that way.

They're really not the same. The right actions are laudable and you're to be commended for going the way you feel most reasonable. But you won't truly be effective until you have trained yourself to think fairly. You must feel fairness rather than analyze it.

You must feel it

This is a very real distinction. On the one hand, you're systematic and mechanical. On the other, you're making the fair decision because it's in your bones.

Acting fair is a great start. It shows your heart is in the right place and your mind is moving in the right direction. But until it's in your bones, you're going to have some reservations about things you must do. Until you really are committed, the chances of underreacting are very real.

You're going to resist some actions you take and not follow through as you should. You run the risk of halfhearted gestures. That's normal. It's tough to do things because you've convinced yourself analytically. When you win an argument with yourself in this fashion, it's hard to really commit yourself to the decision. You, in effect, sigh and go on.

The consequences are that the decision may or may not work. It's pretty tough to hide your own lack of enthusiasm. You may even breed a desire not to succeed in your people. If you do that, then fair isn't really fair. Poor form takes away from what you have convinced yourself you should do. In doing it for appearance's sake you're undermining the very thing you thought you were accomplishing.

Unless you feel it's fair, it probably isn't. You've got to be able to see all sides of a situation. You can't see it as you want it to be. You must treat all people the same and you must view everyone from the same perspective.

Don't kid yourself. If you do, you'll be the only one who is deceived. The people you work with often know better than you what kind of person you are. There's no hiding from the judgment rendered on you day in and day out. You've got to live a standard if you expect your people to accept it. It's not easy, because there won't be anybody there to help you. But you've got to persevere.

Once you really start thinking fairly, your actions will reflect those thoughts. Eventually your people will realize that you not only preach fairness but live it. When that happens, your foundation will be that much stronger.

13 | PULL THE STRING

Millions of managers can plan to do something. Tons of them can see that changes need to be made. The world is full of those who are someday going to make it over.

Shake any tree in the corporate woods and these types will drop by the bushel. They spend hours talking about how it should be or how it's going to be. It's hard to move sometimes for all the people who are going to do so much.

But you know something? Precious few ever actually get it done. They sound so good, so convincing, that you envy them. But in spite of their big talk and revolutionary ideas, they don't produce!

Why? It's simple. It's a hell of a lot harder doing it than thinking and talking about it.

It's no problem for anyone to dream. And that's exactly what thinking without action is. Call them ideas, plans, brainstorms, or anything else you please. The fact remains, thinking without action is dreaming. It's not necessarily bad to dream. That's where many good ideas are born. Many great leaders have been dreamers, but they've been capable of action too.

Dream hero

It's tempting to make yourself a dream hero. You can build yourself up pretty good in the eyes of others. It takes no effort; you can just sit back and talk.

And there's no risk when you dream about doing. What chance are you taking? Where's the fuss or muss? There are no people to push. You don't have to worry about being unpopular. It's easy to see why there are so many talkers and not so many doers.

But that doesn't apply to you, right? You know in your mind what you could do if only the circumstances were right. Maybe, but there are lots of "if onlys."

Any time you are ready to introduce a change there are good, valid reasons on the surface for not doing it. These reasons, by the way, have caused the very top management in many companies to hesitate and not proceed. Listen for them the next time you propose something:

"The people aren't ready; it's just too soon." . . . "It's never been done before." . . . "It's been tried and didn't work." . . . "The timing's wrong, maybe if we wait a while." . . . "It'll cause too much confusion." . . . "It will be too upsetting to the people." . . . "Ah, it wouldn't work anyway."

Sound familiar? Sure, you've already heard many of the same reasons time after time. And you'll hear them again, all those solid reasons that don't hold water. Don't let it happen to you! After you've done your hard thinking and decided something has to be done, do it!

Of course, you don't want to be hasty. There are realistic time factors that must be considered. You must plan down to the finest detail. But untold planners have done nothing but plan. They've planned the plan away. New, rich ideas have been lost because their creators could not pull the string and get them going.

In company after company, plant after plant, countless managers have wished, so wistfully wished, they had done what they had talked about doing. Others talked about the same things, considered the same drawbacks, encountered the same problems, agonized over the same question. Then they went ahead with determination. They overcame the problems and succeeded.

Nothing is static. Development and improvement require constant change. You'll have to make people changes, system changes, custom changes, procedural changes. You'll be concerned with big changes encompassing all your people and seemingly insignificant changes that affect only a few.

But keep in mind that the really profitable changes are those that blend the old with the new. Much of the old is good, even necessary, and should remain. Real progress comes through changes that combine the old into a stronger, better new. These are the true advances that many can see but few can accomplish.

One of the few

You must be one of those few. Once you decide what should be done, commit yourself to action. Establish a firm time frame, not a wish frame. Then discipline your thinking and activity to that end. You'll have to steel yourself against some rugged opposition, but you cannot be deterred.

At the same time, you cannot ignore the opposition. Listen to what others are saying. Don't succumb to their plaints because it looks like the easiest way to go. Don't sell yourself out. But do consider all aspects. Be your own devil's advocate.

Once you make your decision, lay the groundwork thoroughly and carefully. Take as long as you think necessary. But remember, the day of action must eventually come. So pull the string! Implement whatever it is and make it work. Don't worry about the stormy weather. Smooth sailing will come eventually if you're full of resolve. Stick with it and let everyone know that's the way you're going to go.

Just don't make the fatal mistake of hanging on if things go wrong. No one is infallible when predicting how people will react to something new. No one can foresee all the possibilities and contingencies. Don't go down with the sinking ship if you're the one sinking it. It is possible that occasionally you'll have to bail out.

But that's no reason not to go ahead. A chance of failure should be no deterrent. That's always there. If your fear of failure results in inaction, you'll never accomplish anything. As Ben Franklin said, nothing ventured, nothing gained.

You must realize that changes are necessary for the viable plant. It's up to you to make changes, not for their own sake but to strengthen the present and prepare for the future. Once you understand that need, once you have considered all factors, and have made the decision, have confidence in that decision and your ability to give it life.

The world's there hanging on a string. All you've got to do is pull it.

14 | AGGRESSIVE HIRING

You don't have to put up with slackers! That's the gospel. All that talk about having to take whatever comes in the door is nonsense. Pure malarky.

Wait a minute, you say. What about the tight labor market? It's always a battle to get people of any kind, let alone the good ones you really need. Besides, your boss is breathing down your neck. Fill those places. It's all your fault if you don't get more people in there. Sure, the boss knows it's only a numbers game, but it's one the higher-ups are playing too. So get those people by hook or by crook.

It's very tempting to do it that way. The guys up top won't expect much from the effort and it will make you look good. So why not play their numbers game? It might waste some company money, but you can't do anything about that; they're the ones who told you to. If the people you round up don't work out, whose fault is it? Certainly not yours. The brass knew what would happen.

Besides, everyone else has the same problem. No other manager is doing any better. How can you be expected to do something no one else can? You can't be blamed. So why not take the easy way? Who can ask for anything more? Why not indeed! Would you consciously be a party to closing the doors of the plant permanently? Would you turn your back on your responsibility as a manager? Would you do less than is possible and hurt many innocents in the process? Would you readily accept the label of incompetent?

Of course not. But that's exactly what will happen if you listen to those "take anything that ·comes along" voices. As sure as you're sitting there, you'll be sowing the seeds of the plant's downfall.

Not right away, of course. It'll take time, maybe lots of time. A certain amount of inertia will keep the plant going for quite a while. In fact, you will probably experience a temporary surge. That's right, production will probably go up. Everyone will be happy. You'll be the hero. Everything's hunky-dory.

Fall from grace

Then the slide begins. At first it's barely perceptible. But bit by bit, things get worse until you've suddenly got a plant full of people doing less than before. It's true. Be alert to the possibility and prevent it. The world is full of used-to-be plants whose managers still do not understand what happened. What happened was the managers hired warm bodies who had no business working in their plants. And now the plants are no more.

You think it won't happen that way? If you can get more people in the plant, you're going to have more production. Even if they're not all top producers, they've got to contribute something. And what they contribute will add to what you've already got going. It's a natural law, right?

Right! Except that the top producers won't be producing at the top any more. What you once took for granted will no longer be forthcoming. It's a fact. Poor performers pull down the overall level of production. If you let them stay, they will infect your whole operation. The bad will drag down the good. And the very good will be forced out, so the cycle will be turned against you.

You still think that's not rational? Dream on, plantless manager, dream on.

When you accept, even recruit, poor or marginal workers to "fill places," you're on the road to your own destruction. It's not only a question of shouldn't, or theoretically a manager wouldn't; it's what you cannot afford to. If you lower your hiring standards, you've taken the first step in plant suicide.

But, you say, what about the numbers? The boss is still on your back. You need more production. If you've got to have people, you've got to have people! Yes, but not if you destroy yourself in the process. It's a serious point that you have to understand. You do not have to settle for second best and worse.

Go for the good ones

There are still good workers out there. And they're still available to work for you. Even in a tight labor market you can find them. But you must be willing to stick to your standards in order to attract and keep them. You can't hire good and bad workers and keep the good ones. If you encourage marginal workers or nonproducers to come aboard and stay, you can kiss the great new ones good-by.

Now when you hire someone you can't know just what kind of ball of fire you have. Even the most abandoned-looking can be good, and those with promise don't always deliver. You're never 100 percent sure, so in a real tough labor market you might have to hire just about anybody who comes in the door.

Just about, that is, just about. There are some automatics that need not be discussed. And you must be willing to quickly terminate those you hire if they don't work out.

It doesn't take long to know. To be fair you might want to establish a short time period—less than the traditional three months—before elimination. But don't wait too long. Those who do not measure up should be dismissed almost immediately. Otherwise, there's the danger that you'll keep giving them one more chance and one more chance. The longer you let them stay, the harder it is to get rid of them.

Cut the string

So set your standards. Expect everyone to measure up. It may take some people a while to develop, but don't be discouraged. What's important is their attitude, their progress, their efforts to improve. If they make an honest effort, you can afford to encourage them until they make it. If they don't, cut the string.

And you'll be cutting a lot of strings, especially at first. You have to be willing to go through 10, 15 or even 20 to get one that you want to keep. It isn't easy when those turnover figures come in every week, but it's the only way. If you stick to your guns, good people will come by. You might bite your nails waiting, but they'll come if you're patient. Your high standards and advanced thinking will serve as a magnet.

But high standards are not enough in themselves. Good people aren't just looking for a good place to work; they're also looking to make a living. If you expect them to stay, you've got to be willing to pay them what they're worth. They deserve the chance to earn decent money quickly. Remember, they are drawn to a good place to work, but they can't eat stimulation. The money has to be there.

But if the money is competitive, if you stick to your standards of performance, and if you're willing to turn away the nonproducers you can get and keep good workers. You must have a long-term vision to do it. In the short term you won't have much more than your conviction to go by. But you cannot be fainthearted and equivocate. It's one way or the other.

That's a mighty tall order, but it's well worth it. Don't take whatever comes along and be the worse for it. All you have to do is some tough hiring, firing, and managing.

15 GREAT EXPECTATIONS

If you look around your new domain and think your plant potential is poor, you're absolutely right. If you think other managers have an advantage over you, there's no question about it. If in your heart you think someone else could do a better job with the plant, chances are you're right again. With all things considered, if you think you do not have the materials you need, you couldn't be any righter.

You're right because of one overwhelming limiting factor—you. Yes, you. If you have that kind of attitude, there's no way you're going to be successful. The plant will not only do less than it could, you'll probably make it less than it should be. If you think it isn't there, there's no way it can be.

But if you see the potential rather than the limitations; if you can look at your people and see unbounded capabilities; if you can disregard any disheartening initial impressions; if you can see only never-ending possibilities and opportunities, then your plant can and will go anywhere your dreams will lead you.

Your enthusiasm for what can be will be without limit. That's when the plant can soar. Because with that enthusiasm will come your expectations. And your expectations will carry your plant onward and upward. If you honestly believe in the potential, it will be. With that power of feeling you can work wonders.

The key

No plant can rise above its manager. That's the key. No matter what the plant's potential, no matter what its supervisory strength, the manager makes the difference.

This is not a classroom observation. It's one that you surely have seen or even lived. It happens time and time again. The same group of people—not control groups versus testing groups—perform differently for different managers. A plant that is dying has a miraculous rebirth because of a change of managers. Conversely, a high-flying plant hits the skids without seeming explanation after a change of managers.

It used to be true; it's true today; and it will be true tomorrow. The manager makes the difference. And you can bet a major reason is that each manager expects different things from the plant. One expects it not to be there while the other can see nothing but promise.

It sounds simplistic; but it's not. Expectations make all the difference. And great expectations won't come true unless you work to make them happen. No manager can sit in an office, expect everything to be great, never lift a finger one way or the other, and accomplish anything. That's not in the cards. They're your expectations and you'd better do whatever is necessary to make them a reality.

The how

To start with, you must transmit your expectations to your people. Let them know that you have faith in them, that you feel they are capable of rising to the heights. Then tell them exactly what those heights—your expectations—are. You can only lead if your people know where they are going. It goes back to sharing your confidence in them, giving them goals to shoot for and a sense of accomplishment when they reach them.

And reach them they will if they know you not only think it can be done but expect it to be. They will go if you're the one to take them. Are you? Look at yourself. What kind of manager do you expect to be? In the face of problems, how do you expect to get along? How do you expect your plant to do?

Your expectations have to be more than a way of believing; they have to be a way of living. You have to expect more from yourself than anyone else because you know you can deliver. You must feel confident that you can cope with any situation, lead your people through it, and achieve results. You must understand that there will always be obstacles, but nothing insurmountable. It is unthinkable that you will not succeed, even though you realize that success may take a while.

Once you feel it in yourself, you can start expecting great things from others. You see no roadblocks they cannot overcome. You have no comprehension of failure. You lose patience with those who say it can't be done. Because you know where you can go—personally and professionally—and you fully expect to do so.

16 | TECHNICAL PROBLEMS

It's an age-old question: How technically qualified should a manager be?

One camp argues that the manager of a manufacturing facility should have technical know-how to the nth degree. Since managers make the ultimate decisions, they should be able to understand technical problems in depth.

Not so, says the other camp. The manager's job is to manage, not to solve the technical problems that continually come up. Managers manage people and have no time to delve deeply into technical matters.

What do you think? Which way do you lean? It probably depends on your background, your particular bent.

Managers today are pulled from many different areas. There is no one way to move into management and no specialty that guarantees access or success. So where you came from will have a distinct influence on your concept of what managers do and what tools they should have. Training is another factor. When you first entered plant work what you did and who you were involved with exerted influence. Equally influential was the way your first manager handled situations and people.

Now that you're on your own, what kind of manager are you? It's not an idle question. You're a product of your preferences, training, and environment. Your objective now is to be the best kind of manager you can be. You've developed certain strengths along the way and now you must add to them. Even though many different management styles can be successful, you can improve your own. To do so, you must see yourself clearly and proceed from there.

How much do you need?

How much technical knowledge do you need to manage your plant effectively? There's a simple rule to follow. The further you're removed from the operating level, the less technical know-how you need.

This is not to say a generalist doesn't need any techni-

cal knowledge. Every manager should be conversant
with the technical aspects of the plant. On the plant level
good management techniques will carry one only so far.
So if you are a generalist, you've got to get some technical know-how. Don't make the mistake of trying to learn
it all. It's impossible unless you're involved in it day to
day or grew up with it. But do try to understand and
appreciate the technical side.

And you technical people also have to learn. That
detailed knowledge is a wonderful asset. But again, the
further you're removed from direct problems, the less
important that technical function is. No matter how brilliant a technician you are, when you move beyond that
to management, it's a whole new ballgame. You'll be
working with people, and you'll have to learn some basic
management techniques.

Time is a major factor. As manager you really can't
afford to spend a great deal of time on technical problems. Your overall responsibilities are too demanding.
If you concentrate on the technical you'll of necessity
neglect the others.

But, if the manager doesn't get in and solve those
technical problems, who does? Who else has the knowledge, background, and experience to make the right
decision and to determine the proper course?

The expertise

The answer is simple. The people who work
for you. The people who are closest to the situation,
who live with it day in and day out, provide the genesis
of decision making and final solution.

The technical manager says, "But I know more!"

Rubbish. You technical types may or may not know
more. Granted you probably did at one time, but being
away can make a difference. Have there been changes?

Is your memory really that sharp? Do you still have that fine edge? Even if you do, you should let your subordinates solve as much as they can.

Those closest to the problem should be the ones coming up with workable solutions. And they will, if they are given the challenge of the problem and the opportunity to solve it. Forget that you're supposed to know everything and make every decision. You can't always be there. Even when you are, you won't be acquainted with all the facts. The people who work there are. It's their job.

That doesn't mean you shouldn't be concerned if there is a technical problem. If it's serious enough, you're going to have to get involved one way or the other. Sometimes that's the only way the problem will get solved. But you still should give as much general direction to your people as possible. Issue guidelines from which they can work; make sure they understand the parameters of the problem. Then step back as far as you can and let them go.

It's up to you to develop your people and give them a sense of responsibility for what happens in the plant. In cases of extreme urgency you may not have that luxury. You may have no alternative but to take over and say do it this way or that. But these times are rare, and when they do occur you should treat them as training vehicles.

You have to step back. By delegating decisions to your subordinates, you'll free yourself for your general managing duties. Remember, technician or generalist, you are a manager now. And your job is to work through your people.

17 ‖ EVERY DAY IS A CHALLENGE

As you go, so goes the plant. That's a fact you had best acknowledge because there's no getting around it. It's true every working minute from the time you arrive until the time you go home.

Your mood of the moment can set the tone in the plant for the entire day. Your ambition as you approach the day will be a driving force. If even one day goes by when you lack that ambition, you will dampen the spirits of your people. Just get out of sorts for a moment and the reaction throughout the plant will be instantaneous, with a direct bearing on your people's performance.

No time off

It's true. There is no time off from being the boss, although at times you will fervently wish there were. Having a bad day is a luxury you cannot afford. You say it's not fair? Everyone gets down once in a while. Maybe so, but it's something you have to rise above. When you go in each morning it must be with vitality and vigor. It doesn't make any difference how you feel inside. And it doesn't make any difference how often you've done it before. Whatever heights you've ascended, whatever satisfactions you've achieved, are history, even if they happened only yesterday. Each and every day you've got to do it again.

No one can rest on the laurels of previous achievement. It's great that you did it. It's great that your people rose above the expected and performed in the grand manner. But what about today? Even if they did it once there's no guarantee they'll do it again. Things were relatively smooth yesterday but there is nothing automatic about how it's going to go today. No one made a bad mistake yesterday but that's not today. The cantankerous didn't ruffle any feathers yesterday but that doesn't mean they won't today. Just because all problems were solved yesterday doesn't mean some of the same ones won't crop up today.

There's no way that what happens one day will without fail carry over to the next. In fact, once you prove it can be done, or you can produce it, or your people can rise above the norm, you've got something to be measured against. And it's tough to meet that kind of demand every time. But you've proved it can be done, so you have no excuse. Each and every day you've got to prove you're worthy once again.

A new beginning

It's not all negative. Every day also presents a fresh opportunity. The disappointments of one day do not automatically carry into the next. You've had a reprieve and the slate is clean.

Yes, every day brings a new beginning. It's a burden and a strength. A burden because you can never escape it; a strength because there's always opportunity. Either way, it's your responsibility to do the best possible with each day.

What went before is important. It's what you build on, the foundation of where you want to go. Prior accomplishment can be capitalized on. But remember: long, hard, patient hours of productive work with your people can be torn down in no time at all. A little carelessness, a slip of the tongue, a short stepping out of character can destroy what you've labored to build.

You simply cannot afford to have an off day. You cannot let up on your standards. You cannot let emotion rule your tongue or your actions, however temporarily. There's no question that it is a tough assignment, one few could be expected to carry out. There's also no question that it can be done. And there should be no doubt in your mind that you can do it. You have the ability. That's why you're managing instead of someone else.

To do it, you've got to have enthusiasm for meeting each new day. You must look forward to whatever challenge you'll face. You must understand that the satisfactions of today will of necessity pass with the morrow. You must anticipate that whatever you've done is nothing more than a prelude to what you will do. You will have to rise above personal feelings. It's not easy, but you must be so involved that up or down days in the plant do not exist.

Every day you walk into the plant should be filled with anticipation. This is the day that's going to be the best. Even when you're walking into problems, you should see them as an opportunity. No matter what the unpleasant task ahead of you, you've got to embrace the day as a promising one.

It is full of promise. Every day has a freshness of its own that presents a great challenge. Don't let it be any less, for you or your people.

18 | BETTER PAY

It's easy to say "Pay competitive rates." And it's a great idea. There's no question you could get better people by paying more. Too bad it's not that simple.

For one thing, you work within a budget. You can't spend money you don't have. And you might be in a traditionally low-paying industry that cannot compete with others for wages.

So where are you going to get the extra money? The only solution is to stretch what you do have. Make the available money go further. It's not impossible! But it will require time, patience, persistence, analysis, motivation, and turnover.

You're going to have to pay as few people as possible as much as possible, and expect those few to perform. And they will! That's the beauty of it. If you restrict your forces to the producers, you're going to get your money's worth.

This principle is basic to effective and continued operation: give high pay to the performers and low or no pay to the nonproducers or low performers (preferably no pay, because eventually the dead weight must be purged).

Those were the days

Years ago, when labor was plentiful, managers operated under a different theory. There was no question of whether workers were available, but which ones the managers wanted. Because of this bountiful supply, workers were paid low rates. Labor cost was not as significant as it is today. So the common practice was to overload on many jobs. No one was paid very much, but because lots of people were on the job the work was done.

When the boss walked through the plant, people would run or suddenly look busy. The boss wasn't fooled. It was a little game people played, but no one cared because the boss had created the situation and was willing to live with it.

Those were the days! There was plenty of labor, and cheap labor at that.

It's not so any more. The cheap labor that's available is not plentiful. And it's certainly not productive when it is available. You already know that the cheapies will eventually wind up killing you, so you can't afford them in more ways than one. If you hire marginal workers today, the money you pay them is literally thrown away. It's money you could use to attract and pay the producers. It's money you can't afford to lose.

No doubt you think you don't have enough to go after better workers with competitive pay. Your money is constant; your people are constant too. There are X number of dollars and Y number of people and that's it. If you accept what you have at face value, that's true. But you must look beneath the surface. If you're smart enough and want to enough, you *can* take that available money and go after better people.

Do it job by job. If there is an area where three are doing what two conceivably could do, reduce your force. Pay the remaining two more than their current rate and you'll still come up saving money. Look at all areas across the plant. Are you overmanned? Don't make the mistake of judging manning in terms of what you have now. Analyze it from the standpoint of having top workers in every job. Then figure out how many you need.

That puts a completely different complexion on the

situation. Chances are you need fewer people. Then when you look at your available money and divide it among needed workers, what you can afford to pay changes drastically. It is no longer so farfetched to think of paying more competitive wages.

Go and get them

Now you have a concrete plan to work with. You can start going after higher-priced workers. That's when your operation can really start to hum. With better workers all kinds of good things happen.

Production will increase. If you have people who can produce more, and you do your job, they most certainly will.

Quality is bound to improve. The quality of worker makes a profound difference in the quality of the product—another selling point for going after the best.

Absenteeism will go down. Many times it's the marginal performer who gives you fits by missing so much and so inopportunely.

Plant morale is going to improve. Good people feed on and support one another. If you have better people who are earning better wages, your whole operation is bound to be better.

The same concept applies to all positions in the factory, whether they're incentive jobs or those they pay straight time. Get rid of the deadwood and give those who are left some good money.

Making the most of money already being spent should not be your only objective. On occasion you may also need to reduce outlay. But do it in other ways, not by copping out on paying the good, hard-working producers.

When you pay employees enough so that they make money for you, it's money well spent. You spend money

to make money; there's no way around it. That's a must
in any business.

So if you're alert to the potentials in your plant, you
can take the money you've already appropriated and
make it go further. First you have to realize that it can
be done. Then you have to scratch your head and figure
out how to do it.

19 | LITTLE THINGS

You're out in it now. You're talking with people; you're educating your supervisors; and you're starting to get a feel for what's happening.

Employees are finally starting to come to you with
problems, ideas, or just general comments. Not a great
deluge perhaps, just a few, but it's a start. They may be
approaching you directly or through supervisors or
even using a suggestion program you've instituted. It
doesn't matter how; what's important is that they're
starting to communicate.

But, you say, people are coming with items that aren't
very important. Hold it right there! You're talking
about a crucial time—and a crucial lesson for all time.
The little things that people come to you with can make
or break you. They're important to the people in the
plant, they're important to the plant operation, and
they're important to you personally.

Take care of it

Take you first. If you're not on top of the
small things, how are you ever going to get on top of the

big ones? If you let the little things slide, you're kidding yourself about handling the larger ones.

Look at the people you admire in the business world, those who are successful and efficient. You can't help but be impressed with the number of things they accomplish, seemingly without effort, day in and day out. No sooner is a task mentioned than it's done. Not big chores either. The small tasks you wouldn't consider worthwhile they do with gusto.

That's the secret of their success and must be the secret of yours. Take care of the little things. Whether it's a problem in the plant or your office, a request from a community leader or your boss, for your own benefit, take care of it.

Sure, you may hear about the great genius who can't be bothered with details, the brilliant, absent-minded thinker who is concerened only with the colossal. But that's not managing. That's not the way to run a plant effectively. Plant managing is down-to-earth, everyday problem solving and contact. There's no way around it, and if you're looking for something else you'd better get in a different business.

A big part of your job as plant manager is attending to small details personally. Even though you can and should do a great deal of delegating, you'll have to handle many things yourself. How do you stand? Are you on top of the situation to the point where others see you as getting everything done effortlessly? Or are you not? Be honest now.

If you're not, don't despair. It's not a quality that you must be born with. Some people may have a natural bent in that direction, but you can train yourself if you really want to. All it takes is the discipline to develop one simple habit: the habit of doing things immediately, as soon as they come up. When you're confronted with any small task that you need to take care of, do it right away.

Don't throw it in the drawer

Don't let it lie around. Before long the small things will start building. Then, instead of one or two small items you could handle easily, you'll have a mile-long list that will take lots of time—precious time that you suddenly do not have.

Making a note is a good start. But if you pay no attention to the note or just let it lie there, what good is it? You just don't do it. Then, a couple of weeks later, it's still not done and you discover that it should have been. Or maybe somebody asks you about it and you've forgotten and are very embarrassed.

The upshot is you've hurt your community relations, or your personal relations, or—if it's the boss you've let down—your image as a mover. You've impeded progress in the plant or undermined what you've worked hard to build with your people. Tragic, all for the want of taking care of the small thing. Your ideas and visions won't amount to much if the people in the plant do not respond. And the only way those people will respond is to, and because of, your efforts. So they come to you with something small. Small to whom? To you? In the overall scheme of things, maybe. Compared with the big picture, maybe. But to the person involved, it's a critical matter, or you wouldn't have been approached in the first place.

Now it may be only of great concern at a particular instant, and time may take care of it. Or by the time you've reacted it may no longer be urgent. If that happens, shrug it off and don't worry about it. You'll still have shown your workers that you care enough to take time with them.

If you can't, you can't

Always get back to the person involved, whether you take action or not. Always acknowledge that you have considered the circumstance and the employee's place in it. If it's something you can solve with a simple explanation, do so right away. Don't be afraid to say that it cannot be done or that the person is mistaken. It's easy for a manager to hesitate rather than say no to an employee. Don't. If it isn't there, it isn't. That won't hurt.

What will hurt is taking no action at all, forgetting to do it, or appearing not to care. Here you are giving your people this snow job on communication and teamwork, and how important they are, and then not even bothering with such a small thing. It'll destroy you. If you say one thing and act differently, the people concerned will know, and they won't be bashful about broadcasting it to others.

You'll hurt yourself and, even more important, you'll hurt the plant. Because the people are the plant. It's that simple and you know it. If you cheat them, you cheat yourself, and you cheat the company.

Learn to take care of the little things right away. It's a quality that great managing is built on.

20 | FORGET FORTY HOURS

In the modern-day manufacturing plant who has the hardest job? Who is always on call when others can sleep? Who will put in more hours, log more plant

time, and be on the premises more than any other
person?

The manager. Yes, that's the lot of those who would
be manager.

If you think managing is an easier job than what others do, you're sadly mistaken. In order to be the dynamic plant manager who leaps obstacles with a single
bound, you have to forget there is anything like a
40-hour work week. To be effective, you have to be in
the plant earlier than your workers, and you have to
stay later. There's no way around it if you want to do the
kind of job you've set your sights on.

Let's face it, the demands on a manager's time are all-
consuming. It's a fact you'd better be prepared to live
with. Once you've had a chance to organize the plant the
way you want, things may change. But to start with, it's
an all-consuming occupation.

O.K., you say. That's the right philosophy and you're
the kind of worker who will put out and go all out. But
there's no way any one manager can be in the plant
every time somebody's working. That's true. But you'd
better accept the fact that you're going to have to be
there most of the time.

Under normal operating conditions it's not so bad.
You usually can get by with roughly a ten-hour day.
That should give you time to greet people coming in;
time to circulate in the plant during the working day;
time to check everything after they've all gone home;
time to organize and plan for the next day; and even
time left over to do whatever paperwork comes along.

You can do it very nicely by arriving around 6:30 A.M.
and leaving by 5 P.M.—almost every day with no problem at all. Of course, that's for a normal, one-shift kind
of operation. If there's overtime or more than one shift,
the ballgame changes.

Overtime

When your people work overtime you have to be around. They need to know that you consider their work, their extra effort, important enough to be there too.

Even though workers are paid more for overtime, many still consider it above and beyond their normal responsibilities. They may resent it if you are not prepared to go above and beyond too. Or they may begin to wonder why they should stay if the boss never does. Indeed, why should they?

If you have the temerity to ask others to work overtime—and you're the one who should be making that decision—you've got to be willing to work some yourself.

You say it's not fair. You put in more hours than they would ever think of doing. What's overtime for them is routine for you. That's true, but it's part of your job. And overtime is not, in most cases, an integral part of theirs. They don't see that extra you put in daily, so when they're doing more they need your presence as tangible proof that you're willing to do extra too.

It's not a hard-and-fast rule. Circumstances will dictate whether you must be there or not. If you have a dedicated handful of workers or a small, one-supervisor kind of job, you have some flexibility. There are some instances when you can leave the supervisor in charge.

But by and large, if others work later than the norm, you must be there too. If there is Saturday work, you should be working Saturday, just like the other days in the week. You must be there bright and early, stay pretty much the whole time, and say good-by when they leave.

Of course, you don't have to go to the extra trouble. The building's not going to collapse and there won't be

any great catastrophe—on the surface. But you're responsible for everything that goes on in the plant.
There is no way around that fact. You've got to know
what's going on all the time. You've got to supply the
necessary leadership to get things done the way you
want them done.

That's impossible if you're among the absent. You've
got to be there to direct, to lead. So if you ask your
people to work overtime—whether it's early morning,
noon, evening, or Saturdays—you're obligated to work
that overtime too.

Shifts

Shift work is a little different. It's impossible
for one person to cover all hours of all shifts. That's the
reason for shift leaders and assistants and all those
types. There is a physical limitation and you must realize it.

On the other hand, even though you can't be a constant presence, you must be a sometimes one. You won't
get a complete feel for your operation in this manner,
and you won't get as close to your workers as you'd like,
but it's better than nothing. Like it or not, you must
schedule some time in the plant during all shifts, including the graveyard one. You have no choice.

Sure, your schedule is full. In the modern manufacturing world the person at the top invariably puts in the
most hours. The others come in every morning, do their
work, and leave at the end of the day to forget all about
it until the next morning. It's a luxury you don't have.
You carry your responsibility at all times. You may even
be called out of bed during the night. There's no escape.
You have to put in the extra time; you have to make
whatever effort is required.

Time off for you

But don't do more than you should. Don't do busy work just to look busy or form a misguided notion that you have to be "doing" something all the time. If the day ends and there's nothing legitimate left to do, go home. If your routine tour of the plant on Saturday turns up nothing you have to do, go somewhere else.

If you're faced with a mundane chore that is really the responsibility of your subordinates, let them do it. And if some misguided sense tells you to make work that's not there, don't. You're probably just fooling yourself as to what you're actually accomplishing.

Your job is to be there when people are working; it's to be out and around, doing, leading, directing, and motivating. That's where your important work is. That's when you have to be unceasingly on your toes. You need all the sharpness and alertness you can get.

So don't tie yourself to the plant when there's no one there and nothing to do. Take the opportunity to refresh yourself and your mind. Let your thought processes rejuvenate themselves. The old batteries can use recharging, and being away helps.

If you drain your resources by accepting work that you don't have to do, you're cheating yourself and your plant. Don't worry, you'll still have plenty to concentrate on during the 50-odd hours you regularly work each week. Why suffer and burden yourself with more?

21 | LIVE UP TO YOUR STANDARDS

You're the one who has to lead the way. It's up to you not only to establish standards, but to set the example by living up to them. And you must live up to them all the time, not just part of it.

There's the rub. It's hard to do as you should most of the time, but all the time is something else again. After all, a person can only be expected to do so much. Isn't it unrealistic to say that standards must always be lived up to?

Not really. Sure, it'd be nice, but there's no other way if you want to take your plant to its zenith. Now that's not to say you can't let down a bit and still make some improvements. You can probably still get people to perform a little better. You can make some headway in improving production and quality. Yes, those things can happen. So maybe a little letdown on your part really wouldn't be disastrous.

But it would. Any letdown will hurt your operation; any lapse is going to cost some. It may be small and hard to detect, but it's there. Sure, in time you may be able to overcome a setback or two, and you'll probably have to. But a setback is a setback and you'll have to undo it as best you can. And to do that, you're going to have to use precious time and energy needed somewhere else.

You can't let down

That's why you can never let down your personal standards. It makes no difference what area you're dealing in. If the quality of your product is below acceptable levels, you must fix it or not ship it, even if it will hurt delivery and you risk losing an order. If your people are trying their absolute hardest and it's not good enough, you must make them redo it. You've got to hold to those standards even if you feel it's close to passable.

If something in the system you've established imperceptibly starts to deteriorate—a little here, a little there —you must put a stop to it right away. You may think it's so slight and your people are so good and you're just getting to know them. So you let it go, just a little. After all, there's no sense ruffling feathers over something so small. Why stir everyone up or make them mad?

Why indeed! Because you cannot afford to let it slide; you simply cannot. That little slippage will soon get out of control, and before you know it you're crippled.

A small correction early on can save lots of grief later down the road, and it won't hurt your people's feelings that much. They'll take it in stride. If you let it grow, it will become harder to correct. And people will begin to wonder why you're getting so upset about it when it's been all right for so long. Good question.

You can't worry about your people's feelings at the expense of the system. Understanding is all right, but it's got to stop when it penalizes your production. You know there's going to be some fluctuation in production. It's bound to happen because there are so many outside factors. You personally must accept that. But you can't let that acceptance be interpreted by your workers as a lowering of standards. You can understand and empathize to the point where you're figuring out how to get that production back, but it's disastrous to let down on your standards.

Bedrock

The same thing holds true in your human relations. You've been preaching to your supervisors about how lack of consistency will hurt them in their dealings with subordinates. That advice goes triple for you. Your demeanor with employees is critical. That one belittling remark about someone who was not quite out of earshot; that one instant when you were in a hurry and had no time to listen; that one time you stepped out of character—those one times can kill you.

You cannot afford the luxury of letting down. The name of the game is building on sand with people. If they find that you're quicksand instead of bedrock, you're throwing away your time and theirs. It holds true in all areas of the plant, because people are watching throughout. You must honor all your standards that are realistic, and you shouldn't have them if they're not. Consider, if you cannot uphold them, how can you expect others to do so?

It's easy enough to establish standards for others to live by. What's the challenge? How difficult is it to preach about what should be? Not hard at all. The true test of leadership comes when you're confronted with the same temptations. That is the meeting that will make or break you as a manager.

Do you measure up to what you demand of others? Would you give in for the sake of expediency when you know in your heart it's wrong? Have you ever been guilty of overlooking something small because you felt correcting it might cause you more trouble than it was worth?

You cannot afford to operate that way. Your people know. You're kidding yourself if you feel your employees will be taken in. Leading by example is vital. If your words are empty, you will not be followed. If you are not prepared to practice what you preach, you'd better resign yourself to a management of mediocrity.

You must rise above your own frailties. Where others falter, you must not. You must set your standards high, but they must be attainable. Then you must practice what you preach.

22 | OTHER PEOPLE'S IDEAS

Even the best managers need help. In fact, they need all the help they can get. Any assistance, from whatever source, should be welcome.

Admitting that others can help is in no way demeaning. It's no reflection on a manager's ability, intelligence, or competence. Quite the opposite. It's really a sign of strength. The manager who has the confidence to seek outside help is on top of the situation and in control.

It's a fact. No one knows everything. Some pretty smart people will attest to that. No one person can think of every idea that should be considered in every situation. And no one has experienced all there is to experience. No matter the paths, no one has traversed them all.

Expanding your resources

That's why you must learn to accept and use the ideas of others. It doesn't mean that you do not have any. It doesn't mean something's wrong with your thinking. It means you're smart enough to expand your resources.

It's not easy to do that when you start out as a manager. What's easy is to be jealous of your position as boss, especially when you still have to prove that you can run the show. It has to be all your way, because you know things.

You know, for example, that everything must go through you. You are responsible for whatever thinking is done in the plant. It's your job to come up with and introduce new ideas. You may even feel that your people will lose respect if you do not have all the answers. How can they follow someone who is uncertain and goes begging for help all the time? You've got to be the one with the solutions.

Nothing could be further from the truth! You don't have to guard your prerogatives that closely. They're yours and all who work there are well aware of that. The real danger is not taking action because you're too stiff-necked to ask for some good, sound thinking to stimulate yours. If you become immobilized when action needs to be taken, someone else is going to move. For better or for worse, someone will do something.

When that happens, you're in trouble. If you turn your back and let someone else take the action, you have lost authority and standing. Or if you act hastily or in conflict with sound advice because you are bullheaded, you're going to suffer. And your people are going to see your weakness.

Courting opinions and ideas will not lower your standing in the eyes of subordinates. If anything, it is likely to strengthen your relationship with them. It shows your workers you have confidence in them as well as in yourself. And you should have.

Overcoming yourself

Now maybe you genuinely feel that no one else in the plant has anything to offer. You are, after all, the boss. You have your finger on the pulse of the operation. You're not limited in your thinking or ideas by one departmental perspective. The problems that arise are yours to solve. That's why you are there. Who else in the plant is better qualified to make the decisions than you?

No one—and lots of people.

Sure, you've been placed in the position to make final decisions. But that doesn't mean you can't rely on others to help you make those decisions. Perhaps a worker who has been there a long time has experienced the same problem you're faced with now. Or maybe your boss has been through it before. And never overlook your supervisors. Their range of experience in problem solving will amaze you. They may well have been there before. It's surprising what you can get out of them if you put your mind to it. Call on this valuable resource.

Don't make the mistake of selling your people short. It's easy to do if you've been around a little bit more, if you have a more general knowledge, or if you have a better education. But book learning doesn't say it all. The lack of formal education is not always a drawback. There's a lot to be said for just being there. Someone may have had just the experience you need to call on.

So check your employees, your supervisors, your peers, your bosses, for ideas. Have no fear you'll look smaller in their eyes. The only real test, on which you'll be judged, is how the plant performs.

Put other people's ideas to work for you. Treat them as if they were your own. Only the strongest manager would dare to do so; the weak would be too jealous and too ignorant.

23 | TROUBLE SPOTS

It's hard to do some things even when you know the wisdom of doing them. Meeting trouble head on is a prime example. The natural instinct is to avoid trouble, to turn away and hope it will disappear.

That's wishful thinking for the plant manager. When trouble develops you must head into it no matter what. Your job is to solve problems before they grow into big, big troubles. When trouble brews and you ignore it, hoping it will go away, chances are you're giving it license to grow. Then by the time you get involved—and you always will if you're really running the place—it's grown way out of proportion.

The solution will no longer be easy. It will take a lot of time, cause a lot of commotion, and create unnecessary hurt feelings. And there's no telling what other complications will come along. As plant manager, you simply cannot afford to wait. You must react as soon as you know there is something to react to.

That doesn't mean you come in like the last of the Mohicans and start issuing orders, making decisions, and commanding everybody to be perfect again. Once you face the problem squarely, you may decide that no action is necessary. It may not be that serious and may not require your direct intervention. You are training your supervisors to handle such situations and your function may simply be to watch.

The important thing is to be on top of the problem while it is still small enough to control. Unpleasant as it may seem now, it will only get more unpleasant if it goes untended.

The same principle applies when you must take action with your people. You hate to do it. You know it's going to be a dirty job. Still, it will have to be done. There's no escape. You can save hours of grief and agony if you just do it and get it over with.

Foot dragging is eminently understandable. In people situations, you're often faced with doing what you have to do instead of what you'd like to do. Chores like taking someone out of a job, not promoting someone, taking disciplinary action that you know will be unpopular or misunderstood—those moves are tough to make.

You know someone is going to be hurt—someone who you feel doesn't deserve to be hurt. You know someone is going to be disappointed, again someone you hate to see disappointed. You know there is going to be resentment—justified or not—and you hate to have it.

Of course, these are the factors that made the decision so tough in the first place. You spent long hours debating with yourself on the best course of action. But now all the soul searching is over and the decision has been made. It's time for action and you know it.

If you delay, and delay again, imagining all kinds of problems and ramifications, you'll only be punishing yourself. What needs to be done isn't getting done. You're getting an ulcer worrying and you're going to end up doing it anyway. So why torture yourself? Most of the time it doesn't go nearly so badly as you imagined. Get in there and get it done.

Whenever trouble brews in the plant, attack the problem while it's small and you can control it. Meet it head on, take the necessary action, and follow through all the way. You will save yourself lots of grief and get some very surprising, beneficial results.

24 | WORK WITH WHAT YOU HAVE

Management books are great. They can give you insights into managing and ideas for solving problems. And the few that really have meat provide a wealth of material for the manager willing to use them.

Some of the best books use the case study approach. They present real-life situations, with a cast of characters, problems, and alternatives. The manager makes the decisions and everything falls into place, nice and neat.

Of course, there's one small difference between case studies and real life. The textbook writer can use any kind of character and manipulate situations for the desired results. That's a luxury that you do not have. The situations you face every day are never so clear-cut. The answers you must find are never quite so pat. Your decisions and actions never quite fall into place as they do in the books.

No two alike

It's not in the cards for a very good reason: people. No two are alike. No matter how closely two people resemble each other, they are never exactly the same.

It follows that your relationships with different people will differ. Look at your romantic past for proof. Ever become involved with the twin (not literally) of an old love and make the mistake of assuming they were exactly the same? Only once, for sure.

This point is vital to remember in your working relationships. No matter how closely two employees resemble each other in qualifications or background, their potential, their performance, their reactions will never be the same. There's no way to fit your people precisely into what a book would have them do. There's no way you can duplicate with them what you've done before with others.

Your clay

You must make your selection of talent, choices of leaders, and decisions as to whom to develop on the basis of whom you've got. And those you have are by no means always ideal. The clay you must work with is seldom what the craftsman potter would recommend.

Your lot is to do with what you have. Few plant managers are in the enviable position of being able to go out and get what's needed. Finding the ones who can do is a start. You must go with the others until either they develop or their replacements do.

In this position, you'll often have to transmit your ideas to people who don't give a hoot. You have to move people on a wavelength they've never considered, and have no desire to consider. You'll have to motivate those who don't really care. It's a tough job, and there's no cavalry coming to your rescue. But it can be done.

Your plant has as much potential as any other. Your people can perform up to anybody's standards. Your supervisors can be the envy of all who observe. If it's been done elsewhere, it can be done where you are. With long-term vision you can do it. You can mold your people the way you want. It all comes down to your attitude.

So work with what you have. Go with the hand that is dealt. Then play the cards to win.

WORKING THROUGH OTHERS

1 ‖ SUPERVISORS MAKE IT GO!

A basic fact in the manufacturing plant is that supervisors make it go. Good, bad, or indifferent, supervisors are responsible for the day-to-day task of getting things done.

They are the ones with the firsthand contact, the constant communication. They're on the spot because that's the way the system is designed.

You can have the great ideas. You can be the great motivator. You can influence the attitude of the whole. But the back-to-earth truism is supervisors make it go.

Now it's popular to knock supervisors. A favorite criticism is that they're chosen only because they happen to be good workers—not the qualification that should count most. What the critics forget is that many times hard work is the only criterion a manager has for making a decision. And the truth is that most supervisors who are chosen because of their industriousness work out rather well.

So when you start analyzing your supervisors—and before you become completely disenchanted with some —remember they were chosen for some valid reason. Otherwise they wouldn't be there.

At the start you'll have to go with what you've inherited. In time you will develop key people who will share your load, but even then your supervisors will be the ones on the front line. So work with them from the first. Expect them to be capable. Analyze them with potential for good performance in mind, not expectation of failure.

Ask yourself at first, do they seem incompetent because they don't have it or because they have never been developed? Are you prejudiced because they are older and set in their ways? Can you find out why they were selected in the first place? Are there any who should never have been supervisors or who have outlived their usefulness? Are there some who contribute more than is readily apparent?

You have to give them all a chance to show their abilities. You're going to hear all about the onboard supervisors, but you can't take anyone's word for it.

Be positive

First you must believe that they can do the job. Let them know from day one that you expect a lot but that you have the confidence that they can deliver. Give them a challenge and the support they need. Then watch, analyze, and decide.

Some will pleasantly surprise you, if you don't let early prejudices cloud your judgment. Some will disappoint you because they won't be nearly as good as you thought. Some will be clearly out of their element. Eventually you'll have to do something about them, but you can afford to take just a little time. You don't want to tie your hands by making premature moves unless you really have no choice. If that is the case, move as if you know what you're doing and stick by it.

But more than likely your approach will be slow and

steady. Instead of quick and immediate changes, you'll embark on a program of developing the good supervisors, or those with potential, while gradually phasing out the poor.

It won't be easy. You can see where the plant should be going but initially your supervisors may not share your vision. Many have never worked in another factory and have no basis for comparison. They may be intransigent simply because they don't realize how much better things can be. And don't forget the comfort factor. It's easier for people to do things the way they've always been done. The old shoe fits better.

No time to lose

Since it's going to be a long-term proposition, you have no time to lose. Your resources are limited, but your supervisors must be taught.

Your own knowledge and contact come first. Take every opportunity to talk with your supervisors. As you learn about them professionally, explore the best approach for each. It's up to you to get the ball rolling, to give direction, to provide the incentive.

You won't have the time to cover everyone as thoroughly as you should. Even though you're the one best qualified to take the time, you're also the one whose time is most valuable. So you'll have to search for the right openings, forcing them if necessary. Let your supervisors know that you are interested and tell them what your expectations are.

Your goal is to implement that one basic principle: giving as much responsibility as possible to the lowest possible levels. That means your supervisors will be carrying the big load. You cannot assume that they are automatically ready for the load. You have to make sure. Then you have to prepare them for the ever-increasing responsibility. You have to push that responsibility, giving them as much as and sometimes even more than they can take.

It's going to be a long, uneven course. There'll be all kinds of frustrations. You'll want to give up on them. You'll wonder if they will ever show enough interest. They will, so don't give up. One day you'll see that spark of light; then another and another. And those sparks will shine brighter than any in the Milky Way. Because that's your profit! That's what will make money for you.

When your supervisors take hold, assume the fullest responsibility, yearn to upgrade themselves, you're on your way. Now you can really start to work.

2 ‖ DUMB BOSSES

You don't have to be a manager for long to discover that your boss isn't all that smart. It becomes apparent as soon as you have new ideas or obvious improvements that you want to implement.

You know the go-ahead is a formality, so you play it off the boss. You're all puffed up expecting praise for your brilliance, but something goes wrong. The automatic acceptance is not forthcoming. It's unbelievable! You know the idea or change is good; you know how desperately it needs to be done; you know it would really make a difference.

But the boss won't budge. You're either given a flat-out no—which is hard to take—or asked to dig up more information. Or you're questioned on whether you're sure of your conclusions. You're warned that if you follow a path you think is golden, there's unknown danger.

Or, and this really hurts, you're asked if you've thought the idea through as thoroughly as you should have. Have you considered all the ramifications? Is there more to the change than you've allowed for? It's tough to understand. Certainly you've thought it through or you wouldn't have mentioned it. Besides, you're the one on the scene of the action so you know. There should be no question about your judgment.

What's the holdup then? It's simply that the person you're working for isn't all that smart. The boss is too old to appreciate anything new or too scared to do it. Or something. Well, that's possible. It may be ignorance. It may be fear. The world may have passed your boss by. But the truth is your boss is probably much smarter than you think.

Exposure to experience

An unfortunate fact in the manufacturing world is that young, aggressive, capable managers on the way up have little exposure to those who have preceded them. The good ones usually have either moved up in the organization or shifted to another location.

It's unfortunate because many of the problems you face when you're starting out aren't all that new. The brilliant solutions you concoct over some sleepless nights may well have been considered or even tried before. That doesn't mean your idea won't work where once it failed, or that you don't have a twist that wasn't tried before. It does mean that your boss may have valid reason for hesitating. That dummy may well have been concerned with a similar venture in the past!

In big companies especially, where desired contact is less likely, it's easy to get the impression that those on top are scared or unwilling to try anything when actually their reasoning is based on previous experience. That doesn't help you when you know you've got a good idea that's being sat on, but it can give you an idea of how to proceed.

When you're stopped from doing what you want, do a little digging. Find out why. It will probably take some time, and along the way you'll get some pretty vague answers. Often people barely remember why a project or change was rejected in the past, and now their reasoning just doesn't add up. So work to get the truth of the matter. Remember, your purpose is to learn, so don't be impatient. You don't want the reputation of being hard to get along with. You don't want to antagonize people unless it accomplishes something.

Some ploys

Now you're going to have to be devious sometimes, but don't feel bad. The end justifies the means in this case. So try these ploys:

When the boss is in the right mood, encourage some reminiscing about the old days, about the problems encountered and the unique solutions employed. You'll be in for some surprises. Pursue this approach with other people up the ladder. Even when you encounter someone who can't shed much light or is hard to open up, keep trying.

Ask all the bosses beyond your boss about their experiences. If possible, have a drink with those old codgers. Give them a chance to loosen up. Ask some pointed questions. Then sit back, shut up, and listen. You're going to find out that most of these people have been there. It's hard to see it in them now, but they've probably lived as hard as and a lot longer than you.

Conquer your prejudice about those incompetents and learn. Believe it or not, most of them know what it's all about. They know many things you're on the way to learning. Take advantage of that knowledge and experience. There's another advantage to all this probing and learning. Maybe you can find something in their experience that will let you win your fight. If not, you've still gained.

The other side

And while you're doing it, turn the spotlight on yourself. What do your people think about their boss? In your attempt to get things going, how open to suggestion are you?

Do you give your employees the opportunity to suggest changes? If so and you don't go along, do you explain why? When presented with ideas, do you give an honest evaluation or do you let your prejudices cloud your judgment? When you think something needs to be done at a lower level, do you go to that level for ideas? Do you listen to the experience of those down the totem pole?

It's not too soon to start that kind of self-evaluation.

If you're going to move up or improve, you must have the support of the people behind and below you. Sure, you're going to supply the motivation and leadership, but without their support there's not much you can do.

So learn from your boss. Why does the boss turn you down? Is it right? Can there be a valid reason? Have you left something out that should be taken into consideration? Is there a basis for your boss's actions? Is there any correlation between how you're handled and how you handle? Can you learn something there? Almost certainly.

The lesson is to learn from the things you do wrong as well as the things you do right. Don't let pride or hurt feelings keep you from becoming a better manager.

3 | LATERAL RELATIONS

Engineers are dumb. That's an inescapable fact for a plant manager—even if the manager was an engineer the day before. And if they're not exactly dumb, those engineers are sure to be contrary. There's no way around it. Personnel types aren't much better. They live in their own world instead of the real one. Like most staff people, they just don't understand what goes on in a plant. They're more interested in their own little make-believe problems than they are in your real ones.

If the truth be known, staff people are more likely to irritate everyone and get in the way than they are to help. But you're stuck with them. The company says have them, so what can you do?

One thing you can do is appreciate them! Staff people have one reason for being: to help make the company a better, more efficient place to work. They are there for your benefit, and they control a world of assistance that you can call on.

Unfortunately, there's nothing automatic about getting that assistance. The course of line and staff relations is seldom smooth. Personalities are often a major factor. We all know professionals should rise above the petty politics of personalities, but we all know what real life is like too.

Misguided zeal can be a culprit. One department can only see its purpose and drives straight ahead. Jealousy frequently raises its ugly head. In the corporate game the up-and-comers often feel they must take exclusive credit for whatever is done.

The manager's role

But many times, the problem is plain misunderstanding. Staff and line people just aren't sure who is supposed to do what. No one wants to give away anything and people will usually take what isn't theirs first. When that happens, or whenever relations go awry, everybody suffers. And if the plant doesn't get the benefit of support services offered, the manager isn't doing the job.

If the fences between lines and staff are broken, it's up to the manager to mend them. It's not always easy. Identifying the problem is just the first step. Getting it resolved is the real challenge.

After all, you may be dealing with a so-and-so. There are plenty around and some get in staff jobs. Or you may have to deal with someone who's dumb, or misguided, or overly ambitious. There are all kinds. In any case, you must swallow hard, grit your teeth, and try to work it out.

Chances are it will take a while before relations improve. Even in the most compatible relationships between line and staff, there's never complete eye-to-eye agreement. But the effort is well worth it. Staffers can be a tremendous help in day-to-day plant operations. They can ease the burden of the busy manager.

Let the experts do it

Many engineering projects, for example, take a great deal of time—time that a manager just does not have. They are important undertakings and they rightfully belong to engineering. You should certainly follow the progress of a project and recommend actions, but leave the engineering to engineers.

The same holds for other staff functions. You need to know what's going on. You have to be in on decisions and changes. But you cannot physically take the time to handle the routine chores that staff assistance provides for. They've got their thing to do; let them do it.

Besides, being a pragmatic sort, you realize that sometimes those sly staff people get promoted in spite of themselves. Or they get transferred to a place where you can use a contact. In the big, and often not so big outfits, you never know where your contemporaries will wind up. The same people you tussle with today may one day have information or an entrée that you very well can use.

But that's secondary. These valuable contacts will materialize only if you have the kind of plant you're striving for.

Improve those relations

The way to improve relations with staff functions is to understand what they're all about. Learn about them! Find out why the powers-that-be decided to spend money on staff jobs in the first place. Determine how the staff function is supposed to be applied.

If the application now seems to be misused or misguided, find out why. Where did it go wrong and what were the circumstances? Look for the the intended good. From that decide how it will help you. Then if you're not getting the assistance you need, determine how to get it.

You will probably get the best results by cultivating people. If you approach them right, most will respond. Start by being friendly. Don't let a chip on someone's shoulder start one on yours. Ask questions. Find out how staff people view their job, and yours. Seek their ideas on the working relationship between the two.

Ask for assistance. If you have a problem that they can help with, don't hesitate to ask. That's what they are there for, and it can do wonders interpersonally. Be diplomatic. If you feel a person's an idiot, don't let it show.

Be subtle. If you have to give staffers your direction, try not to let them know what you're doing. Be flexible too. If there has to be some give as well as take, do your part. Bend a little; it can go a long way. In fact, you're obligated to go to any reasonable lengths if your plant will benefit.

Now it won't always work. Some staffers will not respond no matter how hard you try. If that happens, you may be forced to draw the line. You may have to say this is my plant, I know what is best, and this is the way it's going to be. When you've got no choice you have to go with what you feel is right. Just don't let that one individual or instance sour you on the system. Keep believing in it and in the people. Don't be the one to let the good get away.

4 ‖ TURNOVER

"Turnover's a killer!" That statement is sure to go unchallenged by any experienced manager. Whenever managers meet to discuss problems, they agree that one of the worst and most pressing is turnover.

Look at the reasons. When you lose experienced workers, production is bound to suffer. It's unlikely that experienced replacements are waiting in the wings, so there'll be a lag between the old workers' departure and the arrival of the new. And when the replacements come, their pace will probably be slower.

Then there's ability. Experienced workers are naturally better because of the knowledge and skill they've gained on the job. Quality will suffer too. New people are bound to make mistakes while learning. Then in the push for production, their error rate will go up.

And how about the cost of training? Even the most conservative experts agree it costs a lot to train new people. When you figure the time, money, and people involved, plus production loss and quality reverses, it's got to be expensive.

In some areas you'll be faced with the bleak prospect of having no replacements whatsoever. They're just very hard to come by because of the intense battle for labor. You'd gladly pay the cost of training if only you had people to train. Turnover here could threaten the plant's very existence. It could be a killer!

But turnover doesn't always have to be a problem. In fact, there are times when it can be beneficial.

Heresy, heresy! Surely turnover's an evil and it must be avoided at all costs. Surely a manager must fight to keep those workers there. Surely, if your plant is full of ideal employees. But can you study your people one by one and honestly say that you could do no better, that you would not replace one because it would be impossible to improve?

Just as surely, that's not the case. If you're stepping into a trouble situation; if your plant is running below its potential; if you're replacing a long-time manager who has mellowed with employees—if it's just a typical manufacturing plant—there are almost certainly employees you need to get rid of.

Some people not only add nothing to the plant's well-being but detract from it. It would be bad enough if they were neutral. But when they undermine what you want to do, when the whole plant suffers because of their actions, those individuals must either straighten up or go!

You must realize from the first that there are people like that. It's up to you to weed them out. They can and will hurt whatever you try to accomplish. There's a hell of a lot to the old saying that one rotten apple spoils the barrel. It will happen if you let it. It's your job to find the rotten apples and prevent them from spoiling the rest.

Who goes?

Some of these people will be easy to spot. You may not find them the first day, but it won't take long. There are several key signs.

Look for those who have a demonstrated lack of hustle. They probably move slowly and tend to stand around doing nothing—until they see you and then rush into activity. Their production rate is lower than average; their quality level below standard. And, let's face it, they're goof-offs. It's easy enough to tell.

So you've found and identified the ones who are doing more harm than good. All you have to do is get rid of them, right? Have your supervisor in charge do it, right? Not necessarily.

Even in the most flagrant cases you're going to have to move carefully. Often these nonproductive people have been with the plant for a long time. They've never done much but they've always been tolerated. Others in the plant may not really like them, may even resent them, but have developed a kind of fondness for them.

You supervisors may question what you are doing and why. They'll know the people you're talking about. They'll agree with your evaluation, even amplify on it. But they've been conditioned to tolerate such people, and you'll have to work hard to convince them that elimination is the best thing. In fact, you'll wind up scratching your head because you're sure to encounter more than one supervisor who agrees that these people are worthless and unreliable, and then balks at removing them because "they're needed."

Discrimination is another consideration. You have to be sure that any action you take is well within the law. You must satisfy legal requirements in regard to sex, race, and age, even when they're not direct factors. Being right is not enough; you must be in a position to prove that you were right.

But even though you move slowly, you must identify these people and get rid of them at the first opportunity. Have a little patience. If the opportunity is too slow in coming, you may have to force the opening for the good of the plant. It will never be easy, but it will go more smoothly if you've laid the groundwork.

Troublemakers

Another group of workers you must watch and analyze closely are the troublemakers. These are the ones who agitate for the sake of agitation. Often they are of above average intelligence and are fair if not downright good workers. They're also pretty sly about what they're doing, so it's not always easy to spot them.

In fact, it can be heartbreaking when you do because often they're the ones who have been the friendliest and warmest to you. But they always keep something going. From one trouble to another, they are found in the center, or at least on the fringes.

Your task here is quite a bit tougher. Many of these people have potential, and you don't want to give up on them prematurely. If you could only harness that energy and talent constructively. And malcontents can be a great source of leaders for the plant. If the negative leadership could just be channeled productively, look at what you'd have. Maybe you can find that key!

You not only want but need to take advantage of the

good you find in these people. Perhaps if you give them the proper direction and enough time to respond, they'll come around.

But—yes, that ever-present but—it doesn't always work that way. No matter what the sociologists say, some people can never be rehabilitated. Their potential is so great that you keep going and going, suffering disappointment after disappointment, thinking always of the next time. But next time never comes. They get so close but never quite make it. Then the day comes when you know in your heart that they're not going to make it.

All that magnificent potential is going to go down the tubes. Your efforts to develop them become counter-productive and you must let them slip away. When you reach that point, you must prepare to get them out of the plant. If they couldn't make it with your almost constant attention, they'll be worse than ever once that attention wanes.

Yes, it'll tug at the old heart strings to think you've failed, but it would be a much greater failure to penalize everyone for the sake of one or two. You'll just have to admit these people are beyond redemption, and you'll do far greater harm keeping them than letting them go.

Pluggers

Another category of employees you'll be tempted to look at are the marginal people. There's nothing special about them; you could even say they were plodders, but they're really not that bad.

The problem is they can't be turned on. They have a set speed and niche and that's that. So it won't be long before you start thinking: If only I could get just a little more out of these people. Then when it doesn't happen, you think: If I get rid of them and get some high producers, we'll really go.

Not necessarily. Remember, brilliant high performers just aren't in heavy supply. The steady workers, the ones plugging day after day, are vital to your continued existence. Every plant needs horses, so don't be too hasty. Stop worrying about these people; you need them. Just make sure you keep them working at their best possible level. Appreciate what they do contribute and live with them.

The hard ones

Another very special group of employees is one you'd rather not deal with, one that will surely test your mettle as a manager. These are the old people who are still trying to work, the infirm who shouldn't be there in the first place.

They are the nonproductive few who you know are a drain on the resources of the plant and company. They are also the ones who couldn't possibly get a job anywhere else if you let them go. So your answer is to keep them on the payroll. No matter what it costs or how much it taxes your margins, you keep them. You keep them because it's your moral obligation.

That's wrong, dead wrong! Granted the last thing in the world you want to do is to let them go. Granted it's a tough situation to face. Granted you could very well lose sleep; you're going to feel like a real bastard; it's one of the most distasteful duties you'll ever have. Granted all these things and many more, you have no real choice.

You have to remove the deadwood from the plant. It's the only fair way to treat your employees, the company, the stockholders, and everyone depending on that plant for a livelihood. No matter how hopeless the situation of the individual seems, no matter how cruel you think termination would be, it has to be done.

You say, "What'll happen to them if they are pushed

out of my plant? Where will they go? What will they do? How can they get along?"

Don't let those questions torture you. There are no answers unless you just happen to know of a job for them somewhere else. And, quite frankly, that's not your concern. It sounds heartless, but it's true. It's just not your concern. Certainly you'll do everything you possibly can, but you'll learn your place only from experience.

These people who you are so reluctant to let out in the cold, who cannot survive on their own, invariably do. You cannot see how they possibly could survive, but they have options well beyond your knowledge. They can and do get along.

So you've really no choice; they've got to go. It doesn't have to be an immediate chop. You should phase it out if possible. But the bottom line is that you cannot carry dead weight. The longer you wait, the harder it is to do and the more clouded your judgment becomes.

There's a moral question involved. Is it fair to endanger the jobs of all others in the plant for the sake of the few? One good-guy exception breeds another. Where do you draw the line? And where's the victory if your exceptions cause everyone to suffer, including the ones you were trying to help? You must go by an objective scale: whether or not the individual is pulling his or her weight for the money received.

Telling them

But you must be fair in approaching termination. Whatever your reason for dismissing employees, you're obligated to give them plenty of warning. They must be made aware of where and why they fall below standard, and they must be given the opportunity to do better. Removal, after all, is the last resort.

So give people a chance to improve. Work with them; let them know you're on their side. If a transfer to another job would help, explore that with them. Termination is much less painful when people know they've been given a fair chance. And most people know when they're not suited. The unpleasantness will never be completely gone, but if you've treated people fairly your conscience should be clear.

You cannot back away from turnover when it is clearly necessary. When it will help production or improve quality, there is no other choice.

Don't shy away because of the numbers. The fact that turnover figures are going to be quoted back to you is no reason to ignore what must be done. Those figures are misleading anyway. Usually a small number of jobs turn over constantly, altering the image of the entire plant. Look behind the numbers. If you have to act, do it even though you know you may be questioned about excessive turnover. Make sure your reasons are valid, then do what you have to do.

And if you have people who are burning to leave, let them go. You might persuade some to stay, but do it with a soft sell. Most of these people have to get it out of their system. So if you can't change their minds easily, wish them well. If they're good, tell them you'll have a place for them and leave that last good impression. Just do your best to find out why they're going. And don't begrudge their return if they reappear. They'll do a good job convincing the others that the grass isn't all that greener.

Turnover. It can be your enemy; it can be your friend. It's up to you to have the courage to determine which.

5 | RECOGNITION

Have you ever considered taking a sales manager's course? That's right, a sales manager's training course. One that teaches you how to get other people to sell things.

The idea is not that far-fetched. Sales managers have tuned promotional gimmickry to a fine art. They generate motivation through a never-ending stream of giveaways, bonuses, trips, you name it. They also use a motivational tool that is less dramatic but even more effective. It's based on one shared human trait—the need for recognition.

The need for recognition is truly a powerful force. That's why big companies with successful salespeople have a President's Club, a Top Ten, or some equally prestigious group. These groups offer extra monetary rewards, but their primary function is recognition.

The people in your plant need recognition too. It's vital for the motivation of your workers and the continued success of your operation. Extra effort should be recognized.

Don't fall for nonsense about how extra effort is really part of the job and should be expected. That's junk thinking. Workers do rise to the occasion. Sure they're getting paid to produce, but that philosophy misses the point.

Above and beyond?

Everyone has a normal pace, a set way of doing things. When anyone goes beyond the norm, that effort should be recognized. And when it is done clearly for the benefit of the company, it should be company-recognized.

Recognition is important not only for those whose heroic effort saves the company; it's also important for people who consistently do the job. They may be pluggers but they are still the backbone of your operation. Or they may be good performers who do above-average work day in and day out, or workers who are making slow but steady progress. All these people need and deserve recognition of their individual worth.

In fact, anyone who is a credit to the company—and that should be just about everybody on the payroll—is worthy of recognition at some time or another. If they're not, they shouldn't be there.

Your people need to be recognized. After you understand that fact and admit that's the way it is, you must start thinking about how.

That's no problem, because the simplest way is the most effective. It's nothing more than a word of acknowledgment, a simple spoken "Well done," "Good job," or "Thanks." These simple words can work miracles. Be on the alert to situations that call for recognition. And teach your supervisors to do the same. Often supervisors are closer to the action and see things that even the most alert manager misses. That's when spoken appreciation, recognition if you will, is a jewel.

Then there's the written word. It doesn't have to be anything fancy, so don't start moaning about having no secretary. A short, handwritten note is fine and will have an effect equal to the finest engraving. Or you can be more formal and get somebody from the front office to type a note, either from you or someone higher. It's not that tough, and it shouldn't happen that often. If it does, it will lose its significance.

Really noteworthy achievements should be publicized. You can print the names of employees and their contributions in your newsletter, on a bulletin board, or in the local newspaper. If their performance is really above the ordinary, why not?

There are many other inexpensive forms of recognition. Use a picture board. Paste up photos of new employees, transfers, promotion winners, and the like. Print or buy certificates to award to employees for training completion, sustained performance, attendance, or whatever you can think of. Print up name tags for people to wear or put on their equipment and tie them in some way to accomplishment.

What about shirts or smocks? If people have a job that sets them apart or one that shows great ability, dress them up. Many companies do this for quality inspectors and even supervisors. If you're on a tight budget, what's wrong with an honored parking place or uncommon or early privileges? How about pins, pens, pennants, flowers, color codes? The possibilities are unlimited.

Time for a change

But keep in mind that as good as motivational gimmicks and programs are, they do lose their punch. After a while people become immune to them. Don't make the mistake of thinking a program is good forever. Even the best will need revitalizing from time to time. And don't get hooked on pride of authorship. Sure you sweat blood over it and it worked, but there'll come a time when it needs a change or it will die.

You must plan all your programs within a time frame. You must decide when to change and how soon one should follow the other. Programs can't be so rapid-fire that they lose their effectiveness through overload. You must pick the time when they will do the most good.

You should also set standards to evaluate your programs. You must analyze your successes and failures—

yes, you're going to have some of those too. If you come up with something that's not a winner, come off it as gracefully and as soon as you can. If you find a good one, play it as long as is reasonable, then put it away to be revived later.

If you decide to use a gimmick, make sure everyone understands what you're trying to accomplish. You're not just playing games. So make sure your supervisors and workers understand your purpose. Provide whatever recordkeeping is necessary and then do as advertised.

Now are you all enthused? Are you ready to spring all this motivation on the plant? Good, but don't expect instant success. You may have the greatest program in the world, but if it's never been tried before, the response may be less than you anticipated. Don't give up. Keep working at it and your people will get the idea. Let your enthusiasm carry the day.

Just remember that even the best motivational tools can do only so much. Personal recognition from you is still essential. That's how you let your people know you know. And, let's face it, you can't beat the cost; you can't beat the simplicity; and you can't beat the results.

Look to yourself. You want to be recognized; you respond to recognition. It's the same for your people.

6 ‖ ASK YOUR PEOPLE

The time is fast approaching when you've got a big decision to make, one that will affect a lot of people.

There are many sides and you're not sure which way

to go. No matter what you do, somebody's not going to like it. So you mull it over and finally start leaning one way. The more you lean the more you're convinced that that's the thing to do. After a while you're certain you are right, but you also know that when you do take action it's going to be a hassle.

That's the last thing you need because it's going to be confusing enough as it is. You want to prevent these hassles. What you're after is a painless solution. Sorry, friend, there's no such thing. Any change is going to stir up trouble. There's nothing you can do to prevent it.

But you can take positive steps to lessen the impact! Whether you have a tough decision to make, an unpopular program to implement, or a simple idea you want to try, you can get help. Help that's right at hand. You can ask your workers what they think before you decide to act.

That's right! Ask your employees, the nonmanagement types, the drones, the pluggers, the people who make your plant a plant. Start with your supervisors and work your way around to everyone. Explain the problem, the reason for it, and then ask for their opinions. Simple? Simple.

But, you say, it won't work! It's great in theory but in practice it will be more unsettling than settling. People in the plant aren't that knowledgeable. They don't have any contribution to make. To top it off, they would probably make you go a way you didn't want to.

Horsefeathers. The time for that kind of head-in-the-sand conservatism is long past. It's counterproductive thinking and you'd better realize it.

They know

In the first place, when something's about to happen, most people are aware of it, even if they can't put their finger precisely on the change. So what you've worried about is already well underway. In fact, the rumors are flying in the most unimaginable ways. Bringing the question into the open will hardly be disrupting. To the contrary, it will help to stabilize the situation. And don't kid yourself about people in the plant not being knowledgeable. Your people survive day in and day out in a world you know little about. They live with circumstances that you're only vaguely aware of, no matter how close you may think you are. Even if you came up through the ranks—a solid trip for many managers—it's easy to forget what it's actually like.

You are right in thinking your people may not understand all the facts. But they know about their world and have some good, sound ideas about it. The people who do the manual work can be invaluable in helping you to consider all aspects of a problem. It's terribly easy to become excited about a prospect when you've studied it from only one side. Employees can give you a better perspective on the situation and can help expand your knowledge. From a purely factual standpoint, you should benefit.

Who is boss?

OK, you say, maybe that's true. But the irrefutable fact is that you're the boss. You don't want to turn your responsibility over to your people. You cannot afford to let them tell you what to do.

You're absolutely right. The final decision should be yours. You can't betray your responsibilities by turning to management by vote. Bleeding hearts and liberals notwithstanding, a manufacturing plant is not a democracy. What you're after is information, not referendum. Control belongs to you and you'd better keep it.

So you're not taking a vote. You're not giving free rein to whatever ideas or suggestions come in, no matter how popular. Even if it's majority by deluge it's not a mandate. So don't give the impression it is. You want other people's opinions; it's up to you to use the information as you will.

What you can do is give the people in your plant a voice in the decision-making process. You can get the help they have to offer. You can get them involved and interested. By keeping them in the know you can increase your own understanding. You can be a pioneer in labor relations, to everyone's benefit.

But in the end you must make the decision, right or wrong; you cannot give that authority to others. The days of the ignorant worker are fast disappearing. The days of the manager as final authority in the plant must never disappear.

7 ABSENTEEISM

It's a killer! No ifs, ands, or buts about it. Absenteeism is one of the worst enemies of the plant manager.

Absenteeism can hurt your operation in countless ways. No matter how fine a group you have in your plant, there's no escaping its curse. It's going to occur regardless of how loyal, how conscientious, or how company-minded your people are. Everybody's going to miss work at some time or another.

It's a fact of life. And if you think the answer to absenteeism is to eliminate it, you're sadly mistaken. It can't be done! The time when managers could know for sure that employees were going to be at work is long since gone. The days when people would literally get up from their deathbed to make the day or labor feverishly without pause are no more.

And people today have legitimate reasons for missing work. You may as well face it. During normal working hours, outside interests sometimes take priority over being on the job. Justifiably so! That's the key. That's the reason you can't say "Be here" and expect whole-hearted compliance.

Time off

Many services are no longer available on weekends or after hours. Medical services are a good example. It's tough to see a doctor without an appointment, and very few see patients on Saturday. If they do, what a mob scene. It's the same with dentists. Try to get a late afternoon or Saturday looksee. Who are you trying to kid? And if it's not a problem in your area, it soon will be.

You simply cannot deny a worker medical attention. Even if it's only for a checkup, how can you argue? If a person has to wait six months for an appointment and a miss means six more months, what's going to happen? Go to work or keep the appointment?

And people really do get sick. When they are, you can't make them work. Then there are family commitments. The kids get sick and must be tended; the spouse is laid up; school officials want a conference during working hours; the mother has never seen one of her children in a school play and this is the last one; or the car stops running and people can't get to work without it.

Good, solid, legitimate reasons.

There's another recent phenomenon. It used to be the husband was the breadwinner and his job took priority. If someone had to take the back seat, it was the wife's employer. It isn't so any more. Many women are moving into key positions that take top billing in the family. It's no longer automatic that the woman is the one to miss work.

The point is people are going to be absent for legitimate reasons. You cannot expect perfect attendance from even a handful. That's the way it is.

It might take awhile to admit it to yourself. You may feel you've come up with the super plant that's not going to have absenteeism. But after you realize you still have it and admit that to yourself, you need to figure out how to reduce it as much as possible.

There are two positive steps you can take to blunt absenteeism. The first is to minimize absenteeism to the fullest; the second is to provide for enough cross-training to have replacements on hand for those who miss.

Make them want to

In the first case, your objective is to get people in to work as many days as possible. The way to do it is to make them want to come to work. Establish a favorable working climate—that's supposed to be one of your projects anyway—so people don't dread coming in. Make your plant an alternative they choose voluntarily.

Start by building a policy for absenteeism based on understanding, and let your people know you do understand. This may take a basic philosophical change for you. You may have a built-in distrust of your workers. You may be convinced they're out for what they can get and will put anything over on you they can.

Put that thinking behind you. Trust people to make their own decisions as to whether their excuse for being off is worthwhile. No more policing or passing judgment. No more knowing what's best.

The only thing you should require is that they let you

know in advance when possible. If they say they're going, as far as you are concerned they're gone, so if you can get them to tell you ahead of time you're money ahead. Then you can plan your reaction. Does that sound too open-ended, too liberal? Is it throwing managerial control and restraint to the winds? Not really.

Most people are going to miss work if they feel they have something more important to do. Chances are they won't get fired for being out once in a while. They can always claim sickness. And when you don't expect them to be absent, you can feel the effects. So if they're going to do it anyway, and you can get advance notice with understanding, get it.

There's another side of it. Many times people have something to do that will take only part of the working day. If they were on the job the rest of the time it would be to your advantage. But they feel they can't come in because of the excuse they've drummed up. So let your employees know that you understand. Take the plunge and tell them they're on their own; all you ask is that they let you know. Encourage them to return to work if they have short-term matters to attend to during the day.

Let them know you feel they're capable of deciding for themselves. Give them the confidence of the company and let them know you expect that confidence to be returned. Go ahead now. It's not that tough and the results will be well worth it.

¡Understanding sí, abuses no!

Besides, you're not going to let them take undue advantage. Even though you're going to let them do as they please as long as they let you know, there are limits. So do not fail to keep records of attendance. That's right, records. Document when they're there and when they're not. Understanding is great and will pay untold dividends, but you must also know who is doing what with it.

Understanding is not the same as tolerating abuse. You cannot condone excessive absenteeism from anybody. That's why it's imperative to keep accurate records. Unless you put it down, you simply can't keep track of it.

Once you start you'll be amazed when you review. Some of your best people will have absentee rates that could be grounds for dismissal if they were less gifted. It's an eye opener. Many times a worker doesn't realize how much time is being lost. Seeing it in black and white can really make a difference. Your good people don't want to take advantage, especially if they know your philosophy is fair.

So don't use the information to chew somebody out. Use it to explain. Talk to people about why you need them. Get some feedback from them to check your standards and expectations. And don't question the validity of their reasons. If you start arguing right and wrong, you run the risk of ruining your policy. You substitute subjective for objective grounds. The only presentation you should make is what absenteeism is doing to the plant.

New managers are sometimes skeptical about this approach, but it will work wonders. Even those you consider hard-core absentees will frequently respond to a straightforward explanation.

If the employee doesn't respond, you'll have to have another talk, this time a little stronger. Make the point that you'll have no choice but to take some kind of action if it continues.

Don't get soft-hearted. In an unusual circumstance you might grant requested absences, but those continuing week in and week out cannot be tolerated. Don't sympathize to the point where you lower your standards. If an exception applies to one, it'll apply to all. And every time you make the exception you hurt the plant.

Should there be no dramatic change after your talks, you must consider sterner action, such as suspension or transfer to a less important, lower-paying job.

Good, productive employees are hard to come by, so you should do everything possible to keep them. But don't bend the rules. Let all your people know they'll be afforded the same kind of treatment. Do what you can to save the wayward, as long as the plant benefits. But if people are hurting your operation, you have no choice. No matter how good they may be, they've got to go.

Termination for cause is a good reminder that fairness works both ways. In the right climate, which you're developing, employees will understand. Other workers usually know before you whether someone should go or not. Just make sure you're fair and you've done your best to find alternatives.

Don't lose sleep over it. It won't happen that often. Good workers will by and large respond. Your confidence in them will result in loyalty back to you. But remember, even your best people are going to miss work on occasion. It's unavoidable.

Protect your flanks

That's why your second task is to build a backup capability. Then when your critical people miss, your operation will not suffer drastically.

It will take a while to do it, so you must start now. Begin by identifying the most critical areas of your operation. Then decide the best way to proceed and do so with dispatch. Do the same in each section of the plant. You may meet some initial resistance, but it's up to you to have the persistence to overcome it.

You'll probably find that the plant has backup depth you were unaware of; most plants do. Your supervisors can help you review and build this backup capability. If you prod a little, you'll find some amazing information stored in the corners of their memory. It will probably come out bit by bit, so keep digging.

And don't forget to look beyond departmental lines. Your supervisors have had other assignments and they can tell you a lot about people in other sections. The talent is there if you go out and find it. Don't rely exclusively on those with experience in other jobs. Some cross-training will be necessary.

And don't skimp on the pay. When you ask someone to go out of the ordinary for the company, you must be prepared to pay for it.

Guard against spreading your backup people too thin. You'll often find one or two who can do everything, but don't assume that's all you need. Your attitude will make the difference. Make it clear to your people that you're working for the common good. Tell them why it's so important that they be qualified to fill in occasionally when someone is absent. Show them how it's to their benefit to have someone fill in for them. Convince them of the need to keep production going; sell them on the idea that quality is a factor. Persuade them that you and the company are on their side. Let them know that reasonable misses are understood and that you're preparing everyone for going that last mile.

Then let them know there will be that last mile.

Remember, absenteeism on some scale is inevitable. There's no way to eliminate it. The hard-line days of "Come in or get out" are gone. But if you're realistic and aggressive you can minimize absenteeism. With understanding and planning you can provide against its crippling effects.

8 | INTEREST

Could you use a gambit for instant communication that would work with anyone? A magic key that would open doors that are apparently shut?

How valuable would this item be if you could get people on any level, in any occupation, to talk to you about themselves, their jobs, the company? What would it be worth to you to have a technique that would establish rapidly and easily that first necessary link with superiors, peers, supervisors, and workers?

It'd be worth a fortune! Just think of what you could do with it. You could move the world and the people with it. Right?

Good, because you've already got it in your power. And it's another one of those little techniques that can do wonders. Very simply, it's showing interest—interest in your fellow human beings! It's the kind of interest that conveys that you care, the kind that lets people know you're really listening. It's a natural interest that makes you want to ask particulars about the person you're with.

Interest can make you a better manager. And it's a quality you can develop. It will take some effort but will return whatever time or work you invest.

There will be some sacrifice, of course. There is nothing easy about these magic little practices. The fact that they are simple has nothing to do with how difficult they are to learn and do. The simplicity comes from the fact that they're available to everyone—everyone who's willing to work hard.

Before you can truly take interest in others, you have to come out of yourself and admit you're not the center of the universe. Then you have to want to learn about people, genuinely learn, not pry. And you have to admit, no matter how difficult it is, that others can make contributions. Yes, others have something worthwhile to say.

You certainly cannot expect pearls of wisdom from everyone, but you can pick up some good ideas on your plant—how it is and how it should be. Even those engineers can help if you're truly interested. So find out what others have to offer.

Sincerity shows

You say that's all there is to it? That doesn't sound very difficult. It's not if you just go through the motions. There'd be nothing to fooling those hayseeds as to whether you meant it or not. They'd never know.

Except it doesn't work that way. The people you deal with aren't naive. They're not fooled by slickness and insincerity. It doesn't take them long to realize when someone is just going through motions. If you don't care, they'll know. And instead of building a bridge, you'll be creating a wall. It happens and it's tragic.

So that's the drawback to working this magic. It must be real to be effective. You must be sincere. When you ask people about their job or family, ask because you want to know. It doesn't have to be a great, in-depth conversation. Once in a while those will happen—and you can really profit from them—but they cannot be forced. If the subject is work, don't expect a lengthy discourse about the job, you're not looking for any great revelations.

And be wary. Some people will try to monopolize your time and conversation. Stay away from them; don't let the few crowd out the rest. You want all your people to know that you care about them.

Job enrichment

You hear a lot about job enrichment. It's a valuable goal for those few who fit into that category. But for the vast majority of your workers job enrichment means taking the time to show you're interested in them.

Some managers have their supervisors keep a record of extraordinary happenings to people in their departments. Then before going into the plant or a particular section, they review the names and make appropriate comments to the individuals. It's a good technique as long as it's not done for the effect alone.

But in a small or rural area, where everyone knows what's going on, such a technique can become suspect. Also, if you get too perfect, it really hurts when you miss. So if you do it, be very good and never miss. Or don't make it formal, but try to get some feedback from your supervisors.

Best of all, train yourself. It's not that tough to be interested if you have the right feeling for your people. You have a tremendous tool at your disposal. It will open the hearts, the minds, and the mouths of your workers. And the replies that come your way will surprise and enlighten you.

It will probably take a little time. People have to see that you are the genuine article, so don't try to hurry it. Let it come naturally. It will if you're smart enough to be really interested.

9 ‖ PATIENCE

Everything you accomplish in the plant must come through others. Let's face it. What could you do by yourself? No superman of a manager could produce what the legions do.

OK, you say. Sure managers need people for production; that goes without saying. But you can effect everything else yourself.

Say you're after improved quality. Well, you can issue dictum after dictum and tell people to do it right, but unless they do it, it won't be done. Or maybe you have this brilliant idea for changing the system. It's going to save, save, save, and the company is really going to benefit. So you draw it up, tell your people to implement it, start living it yourself, and what happens? Nothing, unless the employees start living it too. You can't do it yourself.

This holds true in every aspect of your operation. You can have ideas and write reports and make plans, but accomplishment comes only through people. That's what managing in a manufacturing climate is all about. It means combining the talents of a relatively few to outproduce what that same group could do if they operated independently. It's up to you to bring the diffuse individuals and functions together to create the finished product. It's up to you to make it happen by working through others.

A fly in the ointment

Work through others: You tell them what to do and they proceed. What could be easier?

Nothing, if it really worked that way. But as you sadly know, it doesn't. In fact, one of the overriding concerns of industry today is how to get people to perform as they should. You strive to improve yourself so you can get others to improve. You work to develop your supervisors so they can develop their subordinates. You strengthen the skills and understanding of your direct workers so they will be able to perform.

And they will perform, no doubt about that. All but the poorest will produce in some measure or other. But they probably won't perform to their fullest capacity every minute of every working day.

It's a fact of every manager's life. Even the most trusted workers will at times be less than they could be. Even the closest lieutenant will suffer an occasional lapse. Even the most promising will pull unbelievable blunders that will make you shake your head. You're going to be disappointed, so prepare yourself. If the most trusted sometimes let you down, how can you expect more from those who have less talent and are further removed?

You cannot count on your people being as interested or as conscientious as you. No matter how high your opinion of them, you cannot expect them to feel as deeply or as responsibly for your plant as you do. You have no right to expect as much. You're the one with the ultimate satisfaction. You're the one with the most to gain. And are you perfect? Is there, on the rarest of occasions, the possibility you were less than you should be?

If so, is it not logical to expect the same from others? Of course it is. It's bound to happen. People are going to be less than they should. They're going to do dumb and irresponsible things, especially when you first start developing them.

What's the solution? Finding better people who won't

make mistakes? Replacing those you have with more competent workers? Getting new and different people, like those sharp performers across the street?

Unlikely, very unlikely. That's the one great realization. The people in the next plant aren't any sharper than yours. And there probably aren't any better replacements in your own organization. Unless you have a consistently poor performer, the chances of improving the type are pretty slim.

Winners still are

Your staff, your supervisors, your leaders are in their positions because they have talent equal to and better than most. Those with the shining potential still have it. Those you trust the most still should be trusted. The best of the crop are still the best.

In spite of their shortcomings and seemingly endless mistakes, you can't give up on them. They are still your strength, so you must go with them. It's not a one-shot deal. It's going to take some time, and even then they'll be less than perfect. The only way you will get a crew to meet your standards is to stay with them for the long haul.

So when one of your people is responsible for a gigantic screw-up or gives less than required, contain yourself. Stifle the urge to throttle the offender. If you have to get it out of your system, kick your wastebasket—desks are too solid. Or throw a glass into your office fireplace. Or walk around the building and scream into the wind. Do whatever it takes to get the anger, the judgment-blinding emotion, out of the way. Do anything except take it out on the guilty party.

Certainly it's all right to reprimand or show displeasure. You can't act like Pollyanna and expect subordinates to take mistakes to heart. But you must not carry it to the point of destruction. What have you gained if you vent your wrath, feel better momentarily, but then lose the trust, faith, or even presence of a valuable employee? Good workers are too precious to run that danger.

So go ahead and get to the offenders. Go over what went wrong and why. Don't sledgehammer them as you do it. You and they know who was responsible. Any person worth anything is going to feel guilty anyway, so why cause resentment?

Build up not down

Your best course is to capitalize on the guilt, not by making people feel terrible or worthless, but by turning mistakes into motivation. Work with your people to show them how mistakes can be prevented in the future. While impressing them with your disappointment, display your faith that things will be better.

Turn their thinking the right way, your way. Set them straight on what should be; give them pointers for the future. Then stand aside. If they are as conscientious as they should be, their purpose will be renewed. If your evaluation was correct, they'll be off and running on the right path. You'll be able to sit back, relax, and guide them to greater efficiency.

Until the next serious mistake or letdown or poor judgment, which is inevitable in a training and development situation. So kick the wastepaper basket again, shout out the window, and proceed as before. The same rules apply. Make the best of the situation and use it to teach.

When you're working to get people to improve and reach their potential, it takes lots of time, your time. In the process you're going to discover just how exasperating people can be. You're going to wonder if it's really worth it. It is, so don't give up. Your people will get there.

Keep your cool. Be calm and purposeful. Never lose hope or your determination to make them what they can be. Patience will be your long, strong virtue, one you'll have plenty of opportunity to practice. So do it. It will be well worth your while.

10 || WOMEN, MINORITIES, AND OTHER HISTORICAL LOSERS

Some people resent the federal government's regulating safety conditions, pollution controls, and a long list of other things. If they were around decades ago when wages and hours were regulated, they resented that even more. And those were the same people who fought the unions, and probably still do.

Those people have a new gripe now. As they see it, the government is telling them what kind of people they have to hire. Even worse, it's telling them what kind of jobs to put those people in.

It's not fair. Not fair? Well, not fair to whom? It may make your job tougher, but it's the *only* fair thing for people who have been discriminated against in the past and are now protected by law against discrimination in the future.

If you see these laws and regulations as a burden, consider what you can gain by changing your attitude. Instead of dwelling on what the government has done *to* you and other managers in the country, look at what it's done *for* you. What it's done—and don't be a deadhead about it—is open up a whole new resource for you. You may have just assumed that women couldn't work in certain jobs, and you may have decided not to buck the bigotry of some of your staff. But now there is no other way to go. The government says it must be done. That's a fact of life that is going to be with us from now on.

Your responsibility is to determine how it can be turned to your advantage. The days of fighting it are over. What you must do, and it's critical, is to give up any fruitless, counterproductive resistance to something you can do nothing about and concentrate on turning it into an asset. You have to live with it—use it!

Women

A case in point is sex discrimination. Women have long been members of the workforce and are today a major part of it. Their numbers are increasing and will soon amount to one half of all workers. But even more important than their numbers is the change in their expectations. Women today are looking for their fair share. They are no longer content with jobs that have been traditionally reserved for them.

They believe their talent deserves to be recognized, and if they earn a slot they figure they're entitled to it. Just because a man has always held a position does nothing to deter them. They firmly believe that if they are capable they deserve consideration. They're interested in action and they're going to get it.

There's no getting around the fact that women have

been shut out of many jobs simply because of their sex. It's a fact of life that each manager must acknowledge.

What the new antidiscrimination laws mean to you as a plant manager is opportunity. You no longer need consider only men for positions that a woman can handle but was formerly denied. The resource of capable people has just doubled.

You can now evaluate all your people on the basis of ability. You can concentrate on those with potential and develop them to the maximum. Sheer numbers are going to give you more talent to work with. It's great!

Minorities

Ethnic and racial groups are another strong resource that heretofore has been only lightly tapped in many parts of the country. It's a shame that the government had to get involved to change things (no matter the intentions, government intervention often brings more problems than it solves), but the government has made the opening. Look at the reality: in many places and from many people, there is still much resentment and resistance to the upward movement of blacks. So much so, that it's hard to overcome.

So use the government! If you can't beat them, join them. The government gives you no choice—everybody understands that—so there's your opening. And with that opening, your pool of human talent is once more expanded.

Grab the chance and take advantage of it. It's your only real alternative, so use it to your own advantage. Black, Spanish-speaking, Indian, and Oriental Americans—there are people in these underused groups who have real contributions to make, who have abilities you need. Take advantage of what you have to improve and upgrade your operation.

Don't fall for the tokenism trap. Don't move a couple

of minority-group members or women to positions of seeming prominence and then forget them. If you do, you're cheating yourself and your plant. You're depriving the organization of some very real talent, and you're depriving those individuals of the opportunity to serve. You are cheating the world.

Tokenism defeats your purpose. Developing all your available talent and capabilities is one of your prime duties. So use the government prod as an excuse for doing it.

11 | AGE DISCRIMINATION

The law says you cannot discriminate because of age. People between the ages of 18 and 64 cannot be fired, demoted, passed over for promotion or otherwise treated adversely simply on the basis of age.

It's a good law, in the sense that evaluation of usefulness should not be based on age alone. And that's a needed reminder for many managers. Sometimes managers put too much emphasis on age. They have an ideal candidate for a job in every category, but age stops them and an otherwise qualified person is lost.

Don't let it happen to you. Age is a real and significant factor. But the effects of years vary from one individual to the next. Some "oldsters" are young while some "youngsters" are old. There's no hard-and-fast rule. You must analyze the age characteristic just like every other.

If a candidate for a job has everything you're looking

for except his or her age isn't exactly right, take a chance. You've got a whole lot more to gain than to lose. You're not talking about marriage, so give it a go. It will work to your benefit more often than not.

Old before their time

Now consider the age factor from a slightly different perspective. Consider those people who age before their time, those who do not grow old gracefully.

It's not an uncommon problem. Some people wear out earlier than they should. They literally gave the best years of their lives to the company, but those best years simply did not last very long. Their prime passed early and they can physically no longer perform what they were once capable of. The problem is compounded because these people are still relatively young and need to keep on working. They will be around for many more unproductive years, and they plan to stay with you through all of them.

Well, look on the bright side. They'll probably be there all day every day, with unflagging loyalty to the company. That's fine, but not if they can no longer pull their weight.

If people cannot earn what you're paying them, their loyalty is costing you too much. Your job as manager is to run a profitable operation. If you carry employees without getting the return you should have, you are not doing your job.

But it's also up to you to be fair. That's fair with a capital F, and it's one of the ideals you've come to live and manage by. Is it fair to turn people out in the cold when they've given the company so much? Is it right to turn your back on those who have been loyal over the years and now, through no fault of their own, fail to measure up?

Let's face it. If they can't do the job for you, what are their chances of doing it for anybody? Or even being given a chance? Highly unlikely, and you know it. So you can't just turn them out. You cannot walk away and say "Too bad." Your responsibility transcends that kind of callousness.

But you cannot continue to carry them either. No matter what your heart says, you cannot carry a person who is not performing. It's a disservice to all those who are doing what they are getting paid to do. One exception breeds another and another. That first exception blots out whatever line you had. That's the sure way to destruction. Your plant cannot survive it.

So don't carry them. Instead, find some other work that suits them and pay them accordingly. If they can't perform at past capability, transfer them to a job that will fit their present capacity, with corresponding pay.

Plan and publicize

Don't wait until the day is upon you and there's nothing for them to do. Plan ahead. Make your policy known so there's no stigma to being transferred. It might be hard for the first one or two; but once your policy is accepted, you'll be surprised at how smoothly it goes and how willingly your people participate.

You'll also be surprised at what you can find for people to do. Even in their reduced capacities, many have much to offer. Speed will be replaced by other valued qualities, like conscientiousness. So find jobs they can handle, and make them earn what you pay them.

Cruel, you say? Their standard of living will suffer? They won't be able to do the things they've enjoyed? Their family responsibilities are too great? You'd rather not have it on your conscience?

Well, it may be less, but it's better than nothing. Their

WORKING THROUGH OTHERS   129

pride may suffer, but they won't be killing themselves because they can no longer handle their work. And they don't *have* to take what you offer them. If they truly feel it is beneath them, they have every right to leave. Help them any way you can.

But for the most part their hurt will be momentary. It won't take them long to realize the justice of your actions, and chances are they'll appreciate the lighter workload.

There's no other way to go. You can't assign them "make work." They must have a real job with real value to the plant. That's the only way you can fulfill your obligation to the company and the people in your plant.

If there is nothing they can do, you have no choice but to eliminate them. You can't carry everyone, tempting as it may be. But you're obligated to do your best to keep it from coming to termination.

12 | FLOWERS AND FUNERALS

If you're normal, you don't like funerals. They're gloomy, and sad—not much fun at all. You try to avoid them when possible.

You may have similar reservations about contacting a family that has experienced the loss of a loved one or undergone some personal tragedy. It's hard to know what to say. You feel uncomfortable and the best you can do is mumble. It's something you'd like to avoid if possible.

Don't blame yourself if you feel that way. It's a common feeling, one that's hard to overcome. It's also one that, in your position, you have to learn to rise above.

Whenever one of your workers has a personal tragedy or family catastrophe, you cannot ignore it. Your very position as boss forces you into a commitment. You have to extend your sympathies, and offer comfort, whether it's in your nature or not.

Plant pressure will demand it. Your relationship with the grieving is important, but so is your relationship with the others in the plant. They're going to expect you to do something, so now is the time to provide for that.

Planning

You should establish a policy well in advance. You must consider such things as making personal visits in the event of hospitalization or death. You must determine if you will make it your practice to go to a home or only to the funeral.

You should consider when and to whom flowers will be sent. You must decide who will take care of the details so no one gets slighted. How about the flag—half mast or not? When? Who tells whom to do it? What about the employee's position in the company? Inherently you're going to be closer to your supervisors. Hierarchy in the plant makes a difference, but you must treat those within each strata equally.

And what kind of precedent are you establishing? Will you be able to do for all what you're doing for one? That's the kind of obligation you have, and that's exactly why you need a policy.

You also have to think about the exceptions. What happens when your personal contact with a subordinate transcends the normal? Will others understand that it is not an ordinary situation? What does your conscience tell you to do? What can you afford to do? Circumstances differ, but you've got to anticipate ramifications.

This may sound like a cold-blooded approach. You may not like to think about the misfortunes of others; you may feel it's not an appropriate subject to plan for or even think about. That would be nice. But in the course of events, when you associate with so many people on a daily basis, personal misfortunes are bound to occur. When they do, your conduct is going to be judged with consequences beyond the moment.

People will notice if you do for one and not for others. It certainly will be bandied about if you appear to slight someone. The immediate family may or may not realize it at the time, but they're certain to be told. And it will really be talked about if ethnic or racial considerations are involved and there is the slightest indication you deviated from the norm.

Your place as boss

Maybe you feel you're not that close to most of your employees. You don't know them very well. So not only do you feel uncomfortable and awkward in the situation; you feel there's nothing you can offer.

Well, you're partly right. Unless you are a hometown product or came up through the ranks, there will probably be a little distance between you and the others in the plant. Even so, you can do quite a bit to comfort people by letting them know you care. You don't have to use fancy or grand gestures; just show that you care enough to take the time to make your thoughts known. Simple thoughtfulness will make a great impression.

It means a lot to know that the boss cares. It's worth the effort from that standpoint alone. Don't have any qualms about pushing in where you're not wanted.

Don't worry that you may be out of place or that you may not have adequate words. You must do whatever is proper and consistent.

Proper and Consistent

How do you determine that? Find out what the past practice has been. You don't have to barge around asking what happens when somebody dies; gently feel your way. Talk with various supervisors. Get as many ideas and recollections as you possibly can.

Your next step is to evaluate past practices. Maybe they're firmly established and you can follow the same procedures. Formalize them if so, because you can't take anything for granted.

You may want to change the way things are done. It's up to you. The only caution is that if you do change, do it slowly if possible.

Unpleasant as it is to contemplate, someone in your plant is going to face grave illness, serious injury, or even death. It's up to you to offer whatever comfort you can while not slighting others who may experience similar circumstances.

Prepare yourself. You must do the right thing for everyone.

13 ‖ DISCIPLINE

Motivation is great! The effective manager cannot live without it. You get your people to do exactly what they should, not because they have to, but because they want to. It's a tremendous tool, one that the creative and dynamic manager can use to really get the plant moving.

There's just one problem. Motivation doesn't work with everybody. And those who do respond do so differently, so that there are inconsistencies even among the best-motivated group of workers. This lack of full response can take many forms, from failure or refusal to outright acts of disruption—overt moves against the company, supervisor, or fellow worker.

All these situations call for disciplinary action. It's up to you to decide what kind, how much, when and all the other pertinent steps. It's another one of those unpleasant jobs that has to be tended to. And the final responsibility rests with you.

Without proper discipline you have no plant. Unless all your people obey the rules, you will eventually have anarchy. Another reason you must have plant discipline is consistency. Without control, there's the danger of treating people differently for the same offense. Besides being unfair, you'll be confronted with all kinds of repercussions.

You breed trouble when you are blatantly unfair to some of your people. They know, and everyone else will eventually. Tempting as it is to nail certain offenders, you cannot arrange the punishment to fit the individual.

Another danger you face if you're not consistent in your disciplinary actions is government intervention. Discrimination is the ringing cry throughout the land, and myriad government agencies are ready to take up the cry against an offending employer. You have to walk the straight and narrow. There's no way you can prevent a disgruntled employee from complaining to, or filing charges with, one of the government agencies.

What you can do is insure that each action you take is in line with your previous actions, and with actions taken before your time. So check out the past practices.

If there has been no firm policy, what has actually taken place? Get a reading on what was done when. The policy you institute should not be too far out of line with past practices, unless they were grossly unfair. Then you must get away from them completely.

Be fair and document

The watchword in all your disciplinary actions is impartiality. No matter what you know or who is involved, you must go by the merits of each case. You must establish a program that can be applied to all fairly.

It's also important to document what you have done, the actions that led to it, and any warnings that might have resulted. You must have the proof that you handled each new case the same way you handled the others. Set up your procedure, then make provisions for keeping an accurate and adequate record.

The course you follow may already be established by company policy. Some companies feel the disciplinary code should be very exact. Others use open-ended phrases like "subject to disciplinary action." Whatever your company's policy, you'll still have a great degree of flexibility. Few cases are clearly black and white; the majority call for subjective evaluations and opinions. So you'll be called on for judgments even when the rules are clear and straight down the line.

Actions

There are varying degrees of discipline you can impose. The simplest is a direct talk with the employee. Use this approach as often as you can. It goes back to the idea that you don't hunt flies with elephant guns.

It's to your advantage to keep discipline as low key as possible. You can always use room to maneuver, so you should apply the least amount of effective pressure. Your aim should be correction rather than punishment.

If you need stronger action after one or two talks, consider a written reprimand, something you and the offender know will be on file. You should spell out the problem, how serious it is, the warning being given, and possible consequences if repeated.

An even stronger action is suspension. It should be reserved for more serious offenses and handed out judiciously. When tempers flare for a short period, you may want to suspend an employee for several hours or the rest of the day. Often such a cooling-off period is suspension enough.

Another alternative is shifting an individual to a different job. This can amount to a demotion in terms of money, responsibility, or desirability. If the grounds are strong enough, you can use this technique to rid yourself of troublemakers. Many will leave rather than take the treatment. Just be sure that you're adequately covered and that you keep records of your actions.

The last resort, of course, is termination. If an offense truly merits termination, you have no choice. But don't stretch a point to get rid of someone. If the person deserves termination for some other reason, do it on that basis.

Tell your people

Once your policy is inaugurated, make sure everyone understands it, especially your supervisors. You'll probably want to retain the prerogative of taking heavy action, but you owe it to your supervisors to let them know what they can and cannot do. Make no mistake about it, supervisors must have some discretion.

They have to have some teeth in their authority, whether it's the full load or not.

Don't be caught by surprise. Build a policy ahead of time so that when discipline is called for, you and your people don't go off the deep end. The time for your supervisors to know is before something happens. The time for you to act is after all the facts are in!

14 | MEN AND WOMEN

If your plant employs only one sex, including you, you probably have nothing to worry about. You should be able to ignore most of this chapter.

But it is extremely unlikely that this is the case. Somewhere, somehow, sometime, someone of the opposite sex will be working for you. It's a certainty today because jobs are no longer traditionally reserved to men or women. There are going to be both in the factory.

And when that happens—when males and females spend time together—there's the potential for extracurricular activity. That has been the case throughout the ages and it's unlikely that it will ever change.

Take your own situation. You may think that it would never apply to you. Sure you have contact, but your heart is pure and you are safe. Your moral standards are such that you wouldn't consider a man-woman relationship that wasn't strictly aboveboard. That's great! And you are to be commended, because many people do not feel that way. Or they feel that way only to the extent that it doesn't inhibit them.

The problem is that proximity does strange things to people. The close day-to-day contact between women and men can have undesirable side-effects. What is really sad is that it can happen to "nice" people, people who have no intention of getting involved when they shouldn't. But, unbidden, that day-to-day closeness creates a relationship all its own.

It's a very real possibility that you have to guard against, even when you do not consider yourself to be tempted. In your own mind, your personal relationships with those working for you may be innocent. If you have no exposure or opportunity, you're right. But your own thoughts are not the only consideration.

Purity is not enough

If other people can logically, or illogically, make a connection between you and someone of the opposite sex, they're going to! Even if they don't suspect the worst, they'll suspect something. And they're sure to comment on it. That's the way people are.

So don't fall into the trap. If you have a legitimate occasion to work closely with a member of the opposite sex, don't shy away from it. Often that is a necessary part of the job, and so be it. Many fine working relationships between men and women are strictly professional.

But the truth is one thing. What others make of it is something else. Some people in the plant have nothing else to do but gossip; some are downright malicious; and some genuinely misconstrue the relationship.

Age and attractiveness make little difference. You can be accused of consorting with someone who is too old, too young, too unattractive, or too something else for your taste. It doesn't make the least bit of difference to the tongue waggers. All that matters to them is a juicy morsel of gossip.

Just make sure you are clean. You cannot let an emotional attachment intrude on your working situation.

You must guard against its happening to you, and to the other person. Don't kid yourself and say you didn't see it coming. You didn't notice what was happening until it was too late. And then what could you do about it?

Unlikely, my friend, unlikely. Chances are you saw it coming and either didn't want to admit it or didn't want to take the unpleasant action required. Don't make that great mistake! Be alert to any signs that romance may be creeping in.

Granted it's not always easy. You have to build a loyalty with those you work with, male or female. You have to establish a working relationship that involves a certain closeness. All right, but make sure you keep the physical stuff out of it.

Your great defense is staying clean. That won't stop all the talk all the time. It can still be irritating and may even cause occasional embarrassment. Don't worry about it if you've nothing to hide.

But if you are involved, you are in deep trouble. Both your professional and personal problems will multiply, and you will rue the day of your stupidity. If you stray from the straight and narrow in your working relationships, no matter how careful you try to be, somebody is going to find out. And when that happens, your sins will come back to haunt you.

It's a question not of morality but of practicality. It may have crept up on you. You may not have meant any harm. Your detractors may do worse things than you are accused of. But the fact remains it is a weakness you cannot afford. You must have the respect of your people. If you lose that, the days of your running the plant effectively are numbered.

The man-woman involvement is a killer. Be wary of it.

15 DEVELOPMENT— YOURS AND THEIRS

Your development as a manager should be a thing of beauty, reflecting the classic path of growth. That's the way of the world for all movers. Everyone gets better with time and practice. Experience will make you better, smoother, more accomplished.

As good as you are right this minute, in your heart you also know that you can improve. And you will! As you meet one challenge after another, as you handle one crisis after another, as you solve one problem after another, you will grow. In fact, just going through a period of difficulty will help your development. Your purpose won't be to find a workable solution but just to gut it out. It may not be fun while it's happening, but it's well worth the gray hairs down the line.

Every manager has to face this challenge. It's no put-down on youth or inexperience to say the young have a lot to learn. It's no disgrace to have the experience ahead of you.

The disgrace is to think you're a qualified manager on day one just because you've been given the title. It's a disgrace if you don't realize that you also must develop, from day one on. It's a disgrace if you don't realize that this development is as great a challenge as you'll ever have.

Because no matter how good you are to start with, you must strive to get better. No matter what heights you've already reached, you must anticipate others.

There's always more. And no matter what you know, there's always more for you to learn—or, many times, to relearn. One of the strongest lessons of experience is that we don't always remember what we learn from it.

Your development is of prime importance. You must rigorously pursue it throughout your career. Your success, and the plant's in turn, depends on how well you do and how much better you become.

Judge yourself now in comparison with how you were when you started. How's your problem-solving technique? Do you approach problems a little differently? Do you see problems in a slightly different light? Do you consider the same issues as urgent now as you did at first? Do you delve a little deeper before reacting? Has your procedure for handling problems improved?

And how about planning? Are you a little more thorough now than you once were? Do you anticipate the ramifications a little more fully than you used to? Are you better able to consider all factors because you're more aware of what they may be?

Check your interpersonal relations. Do you handle people differently now? Has your evaluation and opinion changed in dealing with them? Are you influencing them more or are they influencing you more? Which should it be? Have your interpersonal relations improved to the benefit of the plant?

Go through this evaluation process with every one of your responsibilities. Analyze each one step by step to determine if you are getting better. You should be. The problems may not be any easier, but certainly your ability to deal with them should be greater.

Outside help

Much of your personal development will come on the job; that's where the real learning is. But you should also reach for outside support and guidance. Some support will come to you through the written word. Take advantage of it.

Read whatever you can for help—books, periodicals, or flyers. Search out trade publications, including those outside your own industry. If it's a sound management tool in one field, chances are it can be profitably transferred to another. Look to see!

Then move to general writings on industry and working people, anything that deals with human action and motivation. They can give you greater insight into your workers and yourself.

You should also be on the lookout for courses and programs that come your way. If the subject matter is right and the time, distance, and money required aren't prohibitive, take a chance. Even if a course doesn't exactly suit your needs, the experience might be worthwhile.

Visit as many manufacturing facilities as you can. Remember, you're there to learn, not to criticize. Even when you spot something you consider way out of line, don't feel superior. Analyze it. See if there's anything comparable in your plant.

Measure what you see against what you're doing. Look for good ideas that can help and bad practices that may have crept in on you. It can happen no matter how good you are, so keep looking.

Cultivate associations with other managers. Their specific field doesn't matter. They may have some general management knowledge that can help you. You're striving to learn their thinking, good or bad; you are not looking to take everything you hear as gospel. You'll hear many different opinions on the same topics. Get as many points of view as possible so you can make up your own mind.

And seek the better managers. That's where the real

money is. You can learn from people who do it wrong, but you can learn even more from those who do it right. If you're as good as you think you are, you'll see an amazing similarity in the way you all think.

No matter what your philosophy, there are some basics to good management that must be observed. Industry-to-industry differences do exist, but common practices of good management prevail. So get all the exposure you can, from every direction. Others have much to offer. Find out what it is.

Share

And let others learn from you! You've something to offer too. Make it available. Good management ideas must be shared.

Your responsibility as a manager goes beyond the company. Forget the temptation to protect whatever secrets contributed to your success. It's natural to want to keep the edge over the competition. No one likes to lose an advantage.

But the good manager won't! If you were good enough to get there in the first place, you'll have no problem staying in front. The best manager can still outmanage the others, even if it means working a little harder. It's impossible to rest on your laurels anyway. So share!

In a competitive society everyone profits from better management. Managers make the free-enterprise system work, and those who kid themselves that expediency is better than quality do us all harm. The system is strengthened if all managers use the best possible techniques. What good is it to run a well-managed factory if the revolutionaries are in the streets because of the way others manage?

So if you have the chance, help other managers get better. Beat them by being better yourself.

Supervisory development

Keep in mind that supervisory development is a longer- range program than yours. Supervisors do not have the same perspective that you do. They are not as certain of where they are and where they need to be. Their dedication and motivation are not as strong. It's a fact you must live with. If they were as capable and as astute as you, they'd be managing and you'd be elsewhere.

So as you go your way, be alert to ways to help them. As you read for yourself, search for them. When you find something worthwhile, make it available to your supervisors. Encourage those who show an interest to read, and discuss the information with them. Get as many reading as possible, but don't hound those who do not. Some people are simply not readers. Accept that and search for other avenues.

In addition to the reading, look for general supervisory courses that are offered at local colleges, vocational centers, or high schools. Your community may even sponsor programs in supervisory training and motivational techniques. Keep alert to any opportunities.

The no-coercion rule holds here too, although you can be firmer about attending courses than you can about reading at home. Use group pressure and follow-up discussions to encourage the timid to attend.

You can also investigate regional seminars. Occasionally one that's just right comes along in your area, so watch for it. Remember, your supervisors have little chance for outside contacts. Regional seminars can help them build associations with other supervisors.

You must also consider an in-house development program for your supervisors. You can design one of your own, but first evaluate what it takes in terms of time and money. If you decide to use one of the canned courses available, keep in mind that you'll probably have to put a lot of yourself into it to make it work.

Interjecting yourself

Your personal participation is essential in training your supervisors. That's where the real development comes from. Unless your supervisors feel that you're behind their improvement program—expecting it, encouraging it—it won't work. It's up to you to share your ideas with them, to make them understand your expectations and your goal.

It will be a slow, uneven course. But you have to keep pushing. You've no choice. Developing your supervisors is the only route to developing your workers. And without the direct employees, no progress can be made.

Supervisors are the ones who transmit your ideas and goals to your workers—the need for quality standards, the importance of productivity and cooperation, the value of flexibility in the face of ever-changing consumer demands. And your workers are the one's who make or break it. They're the people who make the plant sing as you go through. They're the people who produce the product that makes the money.

So that's your master plan: full development of yourself so you can work through your supervisors; full development of your supervisors so they can do a better job through your workers; and full development of your workers so they can take the plant where you want it to go.

HOME
IMPROVEMENTS

1 | BLANKETY-BLANK INSPECTORS

Inspectors are a fact of life for today's plant manager. You're going to have state inspectors, federal inspectors, OSHA inspectors, boiler inspectors, insurance inspectors, and still more insurance inspectors.

The rule for handling inspectors is simple: you've got to live with them, so be nice to them. There's no question that they can be a pain in the tail, but if you treat them as though they are, they really will get to be.

All inspectors are pretty much alike, except in one way—the particular infractions they look for. No matter how thorough one inspector may be, the next one will look for and find something new. No matter how tight your ship, no matter how conscientious your maintenance crew, and no matter how diligent you are in looking for infractions, an inspector can find something wrong.

Face it. Inspectors are the experts. They make a living going from one plant to another looking for problems that need correcting. That's their job, their reason for being. Do you think they'd submit a report that showed they didn't look hard enough? If you do, you're in the wrong business.

Besides, inspectors aren't really malicious. They just have their pet peeves. That's human nature, so accept it. Don't fret if a new inspector uncovers something. If it's small enough and doesn't involve a lot of money, go along with it. Chances are the inspector is within the letter of the law, and it's better to appear to be going along because you want to than because you have to.

Suffer some nit-picking if necessary. Ask questions, get clarification, try to gain sympathy so you don't get nailed. Do it politely and let the inspector be the expert. On the other hand, if the inspector finds something serious, costly, and clearly unreasonable, you have to resist. Just do so with as little antagonism as possible.

Remember, inspectors are human. They react to how you treat them. So you play a large part in determining what kind of an inspection it's going to be.

Reception

There's no reason not to be pleasant when greeting an inspector. You should be courteous and polite. If the visit is legitimate, don't give an inspector a rough time about admittance just because you know you can.

If you're unsure about the authenticity of the visit, or if your company has a set procedure before admitting any inspector, be more cautious.

Check credentials as fast as you can. If you don't have an established procedure for doing so, get one. Who do you check with and how? What if you can't get the contact? Don't stop asking until you have several alternatives.

While the inspector waits, don't forget your good manners. Keep courtesy and comfort foremost. Blame the rules if there's any delay; offer Coke or coffee; but keep the inspector in the outer office.

If you do have to keep one waiting, don't worry about it. Professionals won't mind if the delay is not unreasonable, and if they think you're doing your utmost to facilitate things. But if you keep inspectors waiting unnecessarily, you'll generate some heat under the collar. Can you blame them? Don't alienate one if you can help it.

The tour

When you go out into the plant, don't make the mistake of trying to hide things that are obviously wrong. Be open and honest about every condition questioned. If you're caught doing something wrong or using equipment that's not technically safe, or if you haven't corrected a situation you were supposed to, say, "Yes, sir."

There's no way out! Don't make excuses that won't wash. You'll cheapen yourself and do more harm than good. It doesn't hurt that much to admit there's something you need to do to come up to standard. Every plant can use some improvements.

And don't try to bluff. You may be pretty smart, but it's awfully hard to con inspectors. Most of them have solid credentials or they wouldn't be looking at your plant. And if the report that goes into headquarters mentions incompetent or ignorant management, you haven't gained too many stars.

If the inspector uncovers something, don't be afraid to ask for recommendations. They won't be binding, and you'll probably flatter the inspector's ego. Also, there's a good chance you'll get solid suggestions on how to proceed. It's nice to believe you're on top of everything, but even small plants are extremely complex. Learn what you can from the experts.

Don't feel that you have to conduct each inspection personally. Some inspectors may get along better with

maintenance people, who often have similar back-
grounds. Size up the inspector before you decide. Many
don't expect the manager to break away to conduct the
tour.

If you do delegate, be certain of the representatives
you select. Brief them on what you're trying to establish.
A good rule is never to volunteer information. Encourage your people to respond to direct questions but not
to overexplain. People trip themselves up more often by
explaining too much than by not saying enough. Don't
worry if the answer isn't complete enough, the inspector
will ask another question.

Review

At the end of the tour most inspectors will sit
down and talk about what they've found. Whether you
participate in the inspection or not, it's imperative that
you be in on the verbal review.

You have two objectives at this meeting. The first is to
find out what the inspector found. The second is to
keep the findings verbal as much as possible. Once
they're in a report, you're bound to action, probably on
a timetable. If the findings are verbal, you'll have more
flexibility. And it's one less document to show up nega-
tively in your file.

Still, you can't ignore recommendations, even if
they're only spoken. If you tell the inspector you'll correct something, you have no choice. Sometimes there
may be more to a correction than meets the eye. If you
can't follow through, keep a record of what you did,
how far you went, and why you were thwarted.

Don't make the mistake of letting the inspector think
friendly, binding suggestions were ignored. There may
be a repeat visit. And the inspector can still make that
nasty little report.

Even if it goes against your grain, you have to meet inspectors more than halfway. They have the whip. It's worth a little bit of crow to keep them from using it.

2 ‖ RAP, YAP, TALK

‖ Educating your people. That's the biggest problem you face. You can generate enthusiasm in your people by being enthusiastic yourself. Others will be carried along by your spirit. It may take a while for the old guard to be imbued with it, but if you stick with it yourself, you'll carry them too. You can also supply your people with motivation. If you work at it hard enough, you'll find the key for just about everybody.

That's great! Both enthusiasm and motivation are worthy qualities and necessary ingredients for your success. But what good are they if the people who have them don't know what to do? In addition to getting your people to want to accomplish, you must give them the tools to accomplish. Even when the ability is there, most of your people will need educating. And that is up to you.

You can't do it through management or supervisory courses alone. These courses, however good, can only supplement the real education that you provide. In fact, many of your people won't profit from a course until they've had the benefit of some instruction from you. It's your responsibility to educate them so they can take advantage of and learn from structured courses. Then it's up to you to get them some. And it's your job to expand on what they learn in a course so that it ties in with their plant duties.

Talking

So you need some method of transmitting your knowledge and learning to your subordinates. There is a simple method, so simple it may not seem worthy of consideration. It's one you can use with just about anyone. The simple tool is talking.

A manager can't always lead by example. Some situations do allow you to demonstrate what should be done, but there are only so many cases that can be exploited. Besides, actions do not always speak for themselves and can be misinterpreted.

It comes to talking, talking a lot. Ideally, you should talk to everyone in the plant. But time is so precious. There is just not enough to go around. You have to decide whom to concentrate on and how to best distribute your talking time.

It goes without saying that your key people should have more of your time. They are the doers, the future leaders in the plant who will assist in developing others. They are the ones you will depend on more and more, the people who will respond better and quicker. They will grasp the significance of what you are saying a lot sooner.

The problem is, if you spend a disproportionate amount of time with these people, others may feel left out. You may open yourself to criticism and jealousy. That's unfortunate if it happens. But you can't be unduly concerned about it. Your key people are your money makers. You have no choice but to spend more time with the few who control than the many who follow.

The next most important people are your supervi-

sors. Some, but not all, will be included in your key
personnel. You won't have as much time for those who
are not, but they are still important. Supervisors are
leaders, and they must know where they're supposed to
lead. You must supply that direction.

It will be a little tougher getting close to your supervisors. Some won't want to talk with you, and those who
do won't always respond. But go after them. Make the
opportunity if you have to. Even with your limited time,
you must talk with each supervisor.

There are other nonsupervisory people who are important to the plant's operation. Identify who they are
and talk to them. Find out what they are doing, and let
them know you are aware of their importance.

Your time grows shorter and shorter, but you still
need to make some available to the direct workers. If
they get the urge, they should be able to talk to you. You
must make yourself accessible. Initiate contact any time
you can.

Who, what, where

But talk about what? Is there a set of guidelines on what should be said to whom? Is there a standard subject matter?

No. What you talk about depends on circumstances.
Who it is makes a difference. Some comments and topics
appropriate for supervisors are clearly inappropriate
for subordinates. Where you are is a factor. A chance
meeting in the supermarket is no time for expanded
commentary on what's happening in the plant.

At first it will be up to you to initiate and guide conversations. Start with topics that are familiar and understandable. Deal with specifics. From the particular you
can generalize. Slowly but steadily you can give your
people the benefit of your experience. Let them see that

their way is not the only one. Let them discover that it can be better.

Tell them how it's done elsewhere. Try to get them to analyze differences between your plant and others. You're a purveyor of experience and knowledge, so expand their horizons. And don't underestimate your audience. People want to know how it's done in other plants. They may not readily agree that it's being done better, but they like to be informed.

You're building on potential. Your people are limited only because they have never known anything else. They have never set any goals because they didn't realize there was a need; they didn't know what else could be. Sometimes their apparent lack of aspiration is no more than ignorance.

It is up to you to supply the stimulus and awareness. Unless you do, you will be thwarted in your attempts to make your plant a better one. It's up to you to bring out whatever promise your people have. You can't do it by preaching, you can't do it by sermonizing. You can do it only by talking, explaining, teaching.

Talk with your people, not at them.

3 ‖ GOALS

Right away, you've a lot of things to do as a new or renewed manager. You're convinced that only a crazy person would think they could all be done, let alone get them started at one time. Well, you not only can but will, because there's no other way.

There's one task you must do at the very first. It's so

elemental that you can make no real progress without. And it's something you will live with for the rest of your managing days.

That all-important something is goal setting. You have to know where you want to go before you can get there. You must determine what you want to accomplish before you can go after it.

Goal setting applies to every phase of your operation: production, quality, absenteeism, rejects, returns, and many others. Any area where you feel you need to attain or maintain a standard is a candidate. Look over your operation department by department, section by section, activity by activity. To improve in any area, you need a definite target to shoot for. It's your job to determine what that target is.

The first step is to identify those areas you are primarily concerned with. (You'll add others in an ongoing process.) Check your current status in each. How does it compare with how others are doing? In some areas you may have to dig to get a handle on exactly where you are. If the information isn't in the form you need, you may have to design a system to make it usable. But the facts are usually there if you look hard enough.

Once you get your information straight, decide where you want to be. Then if you're not there, establish a time frame for getting there. Don't kid yourself; it's going to take time. So project the intermediate steps that will be necessary, steps that may be revised as you progress.

Be realistic

A word of caution here. Don't be afraid to go beyond what you've already done or what you think is possible. Don't hedge just because those working for you have never done it before. Don't back away from what you consider a legitimate ambition. But don't get carried away with unrealistic goals. Don't go after that pie in the sky.

Unquestionably you're going to see beyond what your workers and supervisors do. Your grand plan may be beyond them. But you must give your people realistic goals, ones they can believe in. They must think it can be done.

And be realistic in plotting the time frame. Improvement and progress take time. No manager in history had the magic wand to change that fact. The time will depend on the specific area and where you already stand. So make the estimate as best you can. You won't be precise but you need a guide.

Don't fool yourself into trying the quantum jump. Keep in mind that all growth occurs in cycles. You build to a plateau, rest there a while to establish a firm foundation, then build again during the next growth cycle. If you move too fast, you're going to experience some fantastic but very misleading results. People can be pushed temporarily to extremely high levels, but they cannot sustain them without a solid foundation. When the fall comes, it will be a hard one; and it will be more difficult to resume the building process.

So if there is a long way to go, set intermediate goals. Don't frustrate yourself. You must insure that one building block is firmly in place before you build on top of it.

Two steps forward

Your forward progress will never be completely smooth. You'll move steadily upward in a stair-step progression. You'll push ahead one week only to fall back the next. You'll inch up again only to face another setback. That's normal. Just keep pushing for that long-run improvement.

During these temporary setbacks, and sometimes even during a short upward trend, you're going to think you will never get where you want to go. But if your original analysis was correct, if you gave enough thought and time to determining where you should go, you'll get there. Don't give up just because the road is longer than you anticipated.

You must keep believing, and you must get others believing too. It is vital to get others to share your visions. Many times, even when they want to believe, your people will have misgivings. If they've never been there themselves, or have never seen it done, they're going to have doubts. But each success will dispel another doubt. Stage by stage they will become believers in you and your vision. Their appreciation will grow, and with it their enthusiasm. Keep your belief and others will come to share it.

Sometimes there will be kickers you cannot control. As you're stair-stepping your way, your legs will be knocked from under you. A new style, a cutback in production, a layoff, any of a hundred things can do it. Suddenly you're right back where you began. There's nothing to do but restate your goals and start again. But cheer up, it won't be so bad this time. You're starting at a higher attitude level; your workers know it's been done before. With persistence, you'll reach that first important goal.

When you do, it's time to review. Were you right? Is it possible? Can you go for more? Did you miscalculate? Were there any factors you failed to consider? What have you learned? What preparation is necessary for the next goal? The evaluation never ends. To keep your plant moving, your goals must live too.

Personal goals

And what about you? Personal goals are essential for your own development. You must set your sights on where you want to go. Then you must decide the best way to get there and the stages you must pass through on your way.

Perhaps your personal goal is to be the best plant manager in the industry or in the company or town. Whatever it is, you need to plan and work toward it. If your goal is to go beyond being a plant manager, fine. There's nothing wrong with ambition, so set your sights and work toward where you want to go.

But for the time being your personal ambitions should parallel your objectives for the plant. Your most immediate goal as manager is to get the plant where it can go. That is your reason for being. Even if your final goal for the plant is an intermediate one for you, it must be your primary goal while you're there. It's the one that will unlock doors for you.

So give yourself and your people goals to work for. Lead the way. Don't, under any circumstances, let someone come into your plant, look around, and come away saying, "There's something wrong here. That's a plant without ambition."

4 ‖ COSTS

Self-development is a big part of becoming an outstanding manager. There are many tools you can take advantage of on the way. Excellent primers are the achievements of other managers, those who have been there and have established credentials.

More and more business periodicals feature interviews with top executives—who they are, how they got there, the challenges, opportunities and thinking. These interviews offer a wealth of material. Take advantage of them and read. One thing you'll discover is that every successful executive is concerned with excess costs. They can cripple a company if left unchecked. And they are unchecked many times, because management failed to understand just how dangerous they could be.

A company cannot survive without profit. The greatest enemy of profit is unnecessary costs. It's a drain on the whole system and undermines the foundation of a successful business. A big reason is that the cost is never isolated. When overhead is figured along with the waste throughout the company the cost is magnified. It's true; don't scratch your head. Any cost actually costs more.

It's easy to fool yourself into believing that excess costs are not your concern. After all, for the most part they were established before your time.

Or maybe you feel there's nothing you can do about them; they're part of the system you're saddled with.

You're wrong on both counts. It's your responsibility to be cost-conscious. You must question every item on the expense list. You cannot accept the argument that that's the way it has always been.

Challenge everything

There's nothing sacred about the old way of doing things. Just because your company has spent money for certain items over the years does not mean those items are still needed or desirable. You must challenge each and every expenditure.

You must be equally suspicious of anything new. That first small purchase may be the start of years of unnecessary expense. Be careful of new money you feel must be spent. Challenge your own reasoning. Perhaps there are less costly alternatives. If the expense is necessary, make sure that it liquidates itself when the need passes.

After all, you cannot eliminate all new buying and spending. Some expenses will be well worth it. Just make sure your reasons are sound and not rationalizations. Ask yourself what the return is going to be. How is the money coming back to you? What makes it worth the cost? What is the cost? Where's the money coming from? What factor outweighs the others?

That's a lot to keep track of. How are you to know where the money's going and why? How are you to determine if it's worth it or not? What you need is a tool, one that will help you keep track of available money and where it is being spent. There is a tool, a handy little item called a budget.

Don't turn up your nose. Budgets are not devilish devices invented to torment hapless managers. They're not creations of someone's imagination. They do not require a crystal-ball gazer. To the contrary, a budget is a lifesaving device for the right-thinking manager.

Budgeting is a lot of work. You have to strain the old gray matter because you'll be binding yourself to a performance level. But it's fun too. There's the challenge of matching your performance wits against your projection wits. And cheating doesn't help. Unless there are serious unanticipated factors, it's just as bad to go under budget as it is to go over.

Selling price is fixed in large part on the direct costs of manufacture, and selling price is a critical item. It has to be as precise as possible. If you overestimate to make yourself look good by coming under budget, you're loading the dice in the wrong direction. You could price the product so far out of range that it wouldn't sell.

Then you'd have no production and no star for being under. You must be as realistic as possible. That's where the money will be made.

Even if your company doesn't hold you directly responsible for budgeting, you should get in the habit of doing it. The experience will be invaluable in your daily activities.

Building a budget

Start by investigating records of the previous year's expenditures, whether they've been kept at the plant level or not. Your controller should have them if you don't. These records will be broken down into accounting categories for tax purposes. You should obtain an accounting book for non-accountants as a reference.

If you can't get past history, start a record now. Keep track of where every penny paid out goes and why. It's a tall order but very helpful. In addition to allowing you to analyze expenditures, it will provide a means of comparison.

You can use past or current expenditures as a basis for your future estimates. Not every item will be on the coming budget, but many will have to be. Quantities and usage will provide a guide for projecting future requirements.

Another approach is zero-based budgeting. Start from scratch with every item and base your projections on what you think will happen. The advantage of this method is that every expense is challenged newly each year. But you still need some experience factor to make your projections.

Don't be trapped by the fear of honest budgeting. It happens often in big companies and in government. The fear is that once money is eliminated when it's not needed, it won't be available when it is needed.

If you're faced with this problem, try to be as honest

and as fair as possible. You don't want to hurt your own future efforts, but you want to do what is best for the company. And holding on to money unnecessarily is a very shortsighted way of looking at it.

Life and death

Today many companies are battling for their survival. It sounds dramatic, but it's true. Operating costs are mushrooming. Raw materials are more and more expensive. Fringe benefits are at an all-time high and will go higher. Wages are at an unparalleled level with no end in sight. Profit is getting tougher and tougher to come by. And without profit, there's no company. And if there's no company, how are you going to eat? It's that serious.

As costs go higher and higher, it's essential that unnecessary ones be eliminated. It's vital to determine new and different ways of making the expendable dollar go further. No company can afford to live with waste of any kind.

It's going to be tough. The companies that survive and prosper will be the ones with proper and knowledgeable cost control. And that's your responsibility. It's not up to someone else. You may not have all the control you'd like, but you do have some and you must prepare yourself for when you have more.

So be conscious of where the money is going. Guard against any unnecessary expense. Prepare your budget carefully and thoroughly. You will be doing your part to insure the continuance of your organization.

5 ‖ RECORDKEEPING

Have you ever heard of the Pearl Harbor File? After the surprise attack that brought war to the United States, the military conducted an intensive search for who let the guard down. Subsequently, some military personnel began extensive recordkeeping to make sure that if anything unexpected ever happened again they could prove it was not their fault. This protective device came to be known as the Pearl Harbor File.

What's the connection with you? Why should a manager keep records?

· Managing is a complicated business. It's impossible to remember precisely every decision, discussion, or action that takes place day in and day out. Even if you could, others involved could not. They're bound to remember things differently. Even if you knew for certain, other parties could be just as adamant in their opposing conviction. Whose memory will be relied on? Where's the proof that yours is better than anyone else's? Memory in and of itself is not proof positive.

You need to keep records. Recordkeeping is especially significant today when the charge of discrimination can be raised any time. Age, sex, or race can be a basis for discrimination charges. For that reason alone, you should keep adequate records.

There are other important considerations. You want to be fair—not wanting to hurt anyone unintentionally by going one way one time and another the next. Records can help you be fair with one and all. They'll supply the information you and your people need in determining what policy has been estabished. They'll guide your future actions by supplying precedents you can work from.

Start a file

Records of individual actions are vital. In fact, individual records are so important that's where you should start. You need them and the law demands them.

For example, do you have an accurate record of when each employee started to work for the company? Do you have a list of any breaks in service, along with the reasons why? Do you have current mailing address and telephone number? Do you know whom to notify in case of emergency?

How about the various jobs the individual is capable of performing in your plant? That's valuable, valuable information. Any kind of individual action or counseling should be recorded. You should keep a record of pay increases and of noteworthy accomplishments or talents.

If you do not know how to start a personnel file, or if the ones you have seem inadequate, use one of the standard forms on the market. These may not be exactly what you want, but you can use some parts and let others serve as points of departure.

Policy records

Records of general policy are equally important. Any time you implement a new policy or make a change, you cannot just tell people and hope that common knowledge and practice will suffice as documentation. It must be recorded as completely as possible. You should do the same any time you reaffirm a policy that has never been written down.

Whenever a policy question arises, check to see if there is written guidance. If there isn't, find out what has been done in the past. If there is nothing to go by, do whatever you must and write it down! Make sure your reasons are recorded.

Almost anything you do that affects people should be recorded in some form. You never know when documentation is going to be necessary. Don't learn the hard way. Many managers have discovered too late that they didn't have what they needed when they needed it.

Develop the habit of recording all your actions immediately, when you are in full command of the facts. Until you're caught one time—and that's exactly what you want to prevent—it's difficult to realize just how important complete recordkeeping is. Don't contribute to your own downfall. Keep a record and keep it straight. Document what you've done and why. Be able to prove that you have a policy that applies to everyone equally.

Use the support and fairness that good records can provide.

6 ‖ WRITE IT DOWN

How good is your memory? No problem to you ever? You never forget a thing? Or do you occasionally? Or a little more than occasionally? Do you frequently forget, but just little things? Or, and here's the real kicker, can you remember just how much you are actually forgetting?

Memory is wonderful, but it's also pretty tricky. In fact, it's too tricky to rely on alone when the going gets complicated. As complicated, say, as dealing with the myriad of details and problems you face daily in managing a plant.

There's an old saying that if you take care of problems while they are small, they won't have the opportunity to become big ones. The opposite is also true. If you ignore small problems, they will grow. The day will come when they will rise up and smite you. All for the lack of taking care of a minor detail, a detail you were going to get around to, but forgot.

Don't let pride get in your way or be hardheaded. No one is saying that you are getting old and your memory is slipping. No one is questioning your capacity. It doesn't matter if you are a genius. There are just too many details to keep in your head. To manage a plant properly, you must get involved and stay involved. To stay involved, you must participate in all day-to-day activities. That means you're going to have lots going on, all at the same time. There's just too much to do to trust everything to memory.

Memory aid

So you need a tool to aid your memory. A tool that will enable you to keep on top of many different areas at one time. A tool that will help but not complicate your life. There is such a tool, an invaluable aid that every manager can use. Very simply, it's writing things down.

To start with, you'll need a small notebook and pen. (A pen works better than a pencil because of legibility.) It doesn't have to be elaborate: whatever suits your taste will do. The main thing is to have something that you can carry with you all the time. On the job and off, at home or away, you should always have it.

Then use it. As soon as something enters your mind, write it down. If you make a mental note to remember when you get back to the office, you run the risk of forgetting. If it is important enough to note in the first place, it's too important not to record immediately.

You'll also need a book of some kind. It can be large or small, spiral or looseleaf, as long as it's a book.

Some people write everything down on any scrap of paper that's handy. They've bits and pieces stuck all over the place. They make voluminous notes that are for the most part worthless. Random notes are no help at all because writing it down is only the first step in insuring a better memory. The second step is establishing a system to make use of the information you write down. You have to be able to refer to it regularly. That's why you need a book or something in book form.

Review what's in your book every morning. Look at it every evening before you go home. Take it out before you venture into the plant and when you return to your office. Then move as many items as you can out of your book. Translate your review procedure into action. Get minor things out of the way as soon as possible. If you wait, minor chores will keep building until the list is formidable.

Get the more complicated stuff out of your book too. Make an action list of things that need to be done. As soon as an item is complete, cross it off and update the list. Do the same in your carry-around notebook. Don't let your action list stagnate or be so list-happy that you lose half the things you should do.

Follow through

And that brings up the last step, the very important procedure of follow-through. You not only have to write information and systematize it for review and action. You also have to follow through to see that it gets done. You have to make sure that questions are answered, changes are made, and corrections undertaken.

If someone contacts you personally with a question or comment, always get back to that person. If you don't have time to get back quickly, do it through your supervisors. You'll get them involved and give them an additional opportunity for contact. Make sure questions get answered by making your supervisors responsible. Then follow up yourself when you have the chance.

With all your duties as manager, you need as much help as you can get.

That's why the simple procedure of writing things down can be of such benefit. You'll have a reference to use in initiating and completing action. You'll be able to follow through and stay on top of the situation. Use this technique, to be as good as you possibly can.

7 ‖ COMMUNITY RELATIONS

As a manager, you'll be spending most of your time in the plant. This is especially true in the early stages when you have so much to do to get it going your way.

But you cannot deny the inescapable fact that the plant is a part of a larger world, a citizen of the community where it is located. You have to be aware of that community and, to the extent that it furthers your purpose, you have to make the community aware of you.

Your plant's image in the community is very important. True, personal image counts for something, but managers come and go while the plant remains. Your plant's image has a direct bearing on the numbers and types of applicants you get, on the referrals of others, on the kind of help you get from the town if you need it. It has a direct bearing on your very success as a community relations manager.

Start at home

Community relations begin right in the plant. You must convince your workers that you're a good person and that the plant is a good place to work. Remember, your employees are the real ambassadors. If they believe in you, you'll have an excellent start in the community. Treat employees fairly and the word will circulate.

But you'll also need to get acquainted with the leaders in your town. It makes good sense to meet the people who control your community. You want and need their high regard.

It's really not that tough to get. Unless you're running a sweat shop, you'll be welcome. Any plant supplier means jobs and money, so you're automatically accepted.

Of course, you may have inherited a bad situation. Some managers of the old school didn't care about the town or the people in it. Their feelings were all too apparent and the town resented it. But even in this extreme case the same methods apply. You just have to work a little harder to get the town on your side.

Meet the leaders

Start by visiting the most prominent elected official, probably the mayor. Let the mayor know you're glad to be in town, and briefly describe your philosophy on being a good citizen. Do a little probing. Ask about the local labor situation. Find out about your plant's reputation and any significant past relations. Do it in a friendly and not digging way.

Seek the mayor's advice on other citizens to talk to. Ask about elected officials who may have a connection with your operation, such as members of the City Council or the city manager, if there is one.

The Chamber of Commerce is another good contact. The president will be a prominent, civic-minded official, and one you should meet. Check your company's membership first. If you don't belong, find out why, so that if you're asked to join you have the proper response. Sometimes, local chambers want a company to pay more than the company feels it should. But most will take what they can get, so plead budget limitations if you're recruited. Most companies should and do belong.

Another required contact, if your town has one, is the Industrial Foundation. Its members are frequently moneyed and influential people who prefer to work behind the scenes. They play an important role in determining your competition in the town. Remember, you want the town to prosper, but you don't want competitive industry coming in when the labor supply is tight. If you get members of the Industrial Foundation on your side, they'll feel it's in their best interest to consult with you first. They'll look for industry to complement you as well as protect your plant.

But be fair with them. If local labor is plentiful don't shut out other companies that could help the town. Welcome them for the good of the community and figure out how to outmanage them. If you genuinely feel a new competitor is going to hurt, say so. Just don't campaign against competition because you're afraid of it.

Local businesspeople can also be valuable contacts. A good way to meet them is to join a local civic club. Your town may have several, so be selective. The best one in the town you came from may not be the best for your interests this time. See who's in which. Then go after the one you think is right for you.

Bankers are another valuable contact. If your company has an account at a local bank, start at that one. Put your personal account there and meet the bank officers. Through them you'll gain access to the bank's coffee room, where you can meet lots of the right people.

Then there's the newspaper editor. If anybody in town knows, the local editor does. Every editor likes to be in on what's happening, and you may be news, so you'll be welcome. In turn, the editor may be able to do something for you down the road.

Don't forget the local police and fire chiefs. These two people are vital to your plant's security and well-being. Even though you're more concerned with the people they work for, they'll appreciate the courtesy of a brief visit.

Another excellent contact is the real estate agent. Every community has at least one. And do they have their ear to the ground! This is a contact you should already have. If you haven't lived in the town all your life, chances are you worked through a realtor to find a house. And if you're not living in the community where your plant is located, you're making a serious mistake.

Live where you work

Sure, there are many good reasons for not wanting to move in. The town's too small or out of the way, or you don't know anybody. Well, it's possible to live in one town and be a good plant manager in another, but it's highly unlikely. Unless yours is a satellite plant with tangent responsibilities, an absentee manager is just not as good.

For the sake of the plant you need to be thought of as

local. The only way to get civically involved is by living there. Don't worry, they'll let you in. You're controlling a lot of money that goes into the community so you'll be welcome.

Speaking of money, it's good to spend as much locally as possible. Local buying may not always be feasible because of quantities and availability, but there are some items you can purchase in town. Do so as often as you can. It's good for the local economy and good for you. One local expense you're bound to have is high school yearbook ads. In rural areas especially, kids from miles around are going to hit you for some dough. The same with charities. Any drive in town will solicit the well-financed industry first.

All this is well and good. You have resources and you're glad to help. But it can't be open-ended. You cannot give to everyone who asks. Budget your money. Determine worthy recipients, go with them, and hold a little back for the unexpected. Don't be swayed by the pretty young junior who put on her best dress and most winsome smile so you wouldn't say no. It's hard but it has to be. Once the word gets out that you're a soft touch, you'll have plenty of chance to demonstrate it. And never give in to telephone solicitations from those you don't know. Many slick con artists sound so worthy and so well intentioned that it's hard to refuse. But do it. Ask for a personal or written follow-up. If it's legit, you'll get it. If not, you've saved yourself and the company several dollars.

Community relations are an essential part of being a manager. With all the demands on your time, it will take you a while to get established. But keep at it. Your in-plant progress will be that much easier if the townspeople are on your side.

8 | HIRING

In the old days it was different. Managers would look at the multitudes seeking jobs, choose those that caught their fancy, tell them to report to work and that was it. Incentive was never a problem. Labor was plentiful, and if people didn't work out, they were replaced. The new arrivals had incentive because the word got out pretty fast as to what happened to their predecessors.

Few managers today have that luxury. The numbers and the productivity just aren't there. The net result is that when you hire good people today you have every reason to want them to stay. It's to your advantage to make them want you as much as or more than you want them.

The time to work on their desire to be part of your company is before they even put in their application. Use your reputation as an employer as a drawing card. If you've convinced all the town officials that your company is a good place to work, the word will spread. When they come into contact with people looking for jobs, they'll recommend your plant.

But the town is still a minor resource. The people who really create an interest in your plant are your employees. They are the ones who make or break your reputation with the local labor force. They spend the company payroll dollars and have a ready comment about their benefactor for anyone who listens. They recommend to others whether they should come in and apply for jobs.

So if you're doing your job, many applicants will already want to work for your company. Others will just be looking for jobs and happen to be in your neighborhood. That's all right too. If the potential employee already wants to work for you, strengthen that want. If the potential employee isn't familiar with you, instill that want.

Make them welcome

Do it as soon as applicants come through the door. Make them welcome! Use that initial impression to attract rather than repel. Check your physical surroundings. Is your reception area cold? Unattractive? Even forbidding? How would you feel walking in as an applicant? Would you know what to do? What door to go in? What hours were observed? Where to go once inside?

In addition to making the surroundings warm and appealing, you must let people know what to do. If your receptionist isn't on duty, use friendly, visible, and easily understood signs. Applicants should feel that you expect them, that you were considerate in your preparation and gave some thought to their reception.

Personal contact should occur as soon as possible after the applicant has arrived. This first official contact is critical. You cannot afford to have anyone just go through the motions in greeting prospective employees. A warm welcome can overcome the most barren physical surroundings. A poor welcome can negate the brightest, best-planned room. That's why a regular receptionist is a must. If a warm and enthusiastic welcome results, it's time and money well spent.

That enthusiasm should be matched with efficiency. Set up a procedure that your receptionist can follow with everyone. Make sure materials are always handy. Don't keep people waiting unnecessarily with an ill-timed search for blanks, pencils, clipboards, or whatever. Let the applicants know you are aware of their presence, and make sure the next contact doesn't take forever.

When they ask about the hiring situation, don't be coy. If there's not much chance, say so. If you are hiring only experienced—truly experienced—workers, let them know. Level with the applicants. Tell the truth and tell it the same way to one and all.

Keep the application blank as simple and short as possible. Go for a minimum of details. You don't need a life history. Figure out what information you need. Just make sure all questions are within the law.

Don't delay

Take applications with dispatch. Don't delay. Time's too valuable to waste. If your receptionist gets swamped, a trained assistant should be standing by to lend a hand. Be prepared for the unexpected.

If you're giving prehire interviews or tests, try to do so while the applicants are there. Don't have them coming back for no reason. Why waste their time or yours?

How's it possible? Simple. Nobody says you have to take applications at a candidate's convenience. Take them at yours. And have yours when a qualified interviewer is available. The person who will actually do the hiring should conduct the interviews if possible, again in the interest of saving time. Make sure the interviewer has a checklist, so that every point gets covered and every applicant is treated alike.

Of course, if there is a large number of applicants, interviews may not be possible. And in more sensitive positions several interviews may be necessary. Just make sure you don't drag the rejection process out. It's to everybody's advantage to reduce dead time.

Your plant's image is based in part on the consideration you show to everyone, even your rejects. So be the warm, friendly, honest company to one and all. If you do, those applicants will keep coming.

9 ‖ QUALITY

The president of a very successful company once said, "If we had to make a choice between quality and production, we'd take quality."

That was a very sincere statement, one that the man felt and preached. There was nothing hypocritical about it and no one listening felt there was. But several plant managers in that company have been removed because of poor production, while precious few, if any, have been axed because of poor quality.

You've probably heard other company leaders say basically the same thing. It's quality this and quality that, but when it comes to the crunch, it's production that counts. It makes you wonder. Do these people really believe that quality is important or are they just paying lip service to the idea? Does, in fact, quality matter?

Yes, it does. Quality has always been important. It's important now and will continue to be important in the future. As a manager, don't make the mistake of thinking that the top people don't mean it when they say they are concerned about quality. True, you probably won't get fired if you can get out the production and your quality lacks a little. But a noticeable trend of poor quality will bring you some unpleasant letters and phone calls.

But that's beside the point. What counts is quality. Your company wants it. The customer wants it. And you, above all, should want it.

The problem is determining just what the word "quality" means. Many people preach "quality"; papers are written on the need for "quality." But seldom is the word defined. Because it can't be. Quality is not an absolute, although people treat it as such. There are different quality levels for different markets and even within markets. To complicate things, the level within any particular market can change completely, if only temporarily.

The fickle consumer

That's one reason quality standards seem less important when production demands are high. When people are in a buying mood, they'll buy! They don't want to wait. They want what they want now and the reason for this mood is seldom quality. In fact, during a real strong buying spree quality pales in importance.

In essence the public has lowered its quality standards. The company is not so much changing standards as acquiescing to buyer demand. If you don't ship, they don't buy. If they don't buy, you don't make money. If you don't make money, you don't exist. Likewise your customer, the retailer, has changed standards. It doesn't matter what you ship as long as it sells. That's what it's all about. It can't be sold if it's not in the store.

The boom ends. It always does. The time comes when normal buying habits take over. People get tired of the style or have as much as they need. Or there's an economic downturn. All of a sudden the stuff's not walking out of the stores.

So it's there to look at. The retailers have plenty of opportunity to examine it. And lo and behold, the astute retailer finds some poor workmanship. There it is, no question about it. No wonder the product is no longer selling. It's the manufacturer's fault. If one or two store customers have returned an inferior product, so much the better. There's nothing left to do but send it back.

And if the customer is a good one, you will take it back, even if you suspect that the retailer is just reducing inventory the painless way. You've no choice. If your company is a reliable supplier—and it should be—you're beholden to make good on shoddy workmanship. You've got to take the junk back.

So the powers-that-be suddenly see all these returns. They check, and, sure enough, there it is: bad quality. Certainly it's not up to company standards. Better tighten up again. You get that, manager?

Yes, sir. But . . .

That's enough! Stop right there. Don't say *they* said ship. Even if it's true that's no excuse. Your job is to ship the kind of quality that your customers paid for, even if quality wasn't their primary consideration at the time.

Quality defined

And that's your definition of quality. Your standard is the best possible workmanship and materials the customer can expect for the money paid. That must be the basis of any quality control program. You must know what the customer is paying for. Then you must transmit that to your people. Once they understand, you can attain the quality level you're after.

There are just about as many kinds of quality control programs as there are companies. They're formal, informal, statistical, extensive, limited. If your company has one, you must see that it's used properly and effectively. If none is in being, you must design one. It doesn't have to be complicated. A little informal record-keeping can do wonders. And it shouldn't be an end in itself. It's a tool, nothing more.

Get your supervisors involved. Let them know what you're after and why. You have to put the responsibility on them, because that's where the impetus comes from. Even the most sophisticated quality control program is based on checking what has been done. So to get the desired results, you must make sure your supervisors emphasize putting the quality in during the manufacturing process.

Your attitude is the key. You must let your supervisors know that you care about quality and get them to care; then you must make sure all your people realize its importance and get them to care. When people realize that you will not accept less than standard, quality will become meaningful to everyone.

And when production is pushed you cannot relax your vigilance. Even if you must hire and train new workers, you cannot sacrifice quality for speed or expediency. You have to make sure that new workers learn your quality standards. No matter what the outside pressures, quality remains your responsibility. The customer may be the final inspector, but you should be the most exacting one.

Know the quality level you're shooting for and keep driving until you get there. Then work your tail off to stay there.

10 | ENVIRONMENT

Ecology nuts are something else. All they do is complain. Clean up the environment! Don't litter! Quit polluting! Keep the world bright and the sun shining through!

All that crazy chatter, and for what? Who cares what they're talking about? Not you? Well, no more, my friend. If you're not ecology-minded already, you need to be.

Let's face it, the plant is your employees' world. They spend well over a third of their waking hours in the confines of your facility. Frightening, isn't it, to think that people's lives are so wrapped up in the world you're providing?

What kind of world is it? Is it light, clean, airy? Does the spirit soar on entering? Is it the kind of place that others admire and want to be in? Is it physically and mentally stimulating? Is it the kind of place you want for your people? If it's not, you'd better start figuring out a way to get it there.

Sure, there are arguments against it. It's a factory, after all. People should expect to have some undesirable conditions. A factory can only be so clean and can be kept only so tidy when it's operating. Things may get a little cluttered, but there's just so much space available. And maybe the paint is a little drab, but you need a functional color that doesn't show dirt. Besides, what does it matter?

It makes a difference

It matters a lot. Your physical plant makes a difference in the kind of people you attract and hold. It makes a difference in the morale and attitude of those working there. It makes a difference in how the work is performed. And, most important, it makes a difference in the quality of the end product.

Environment influences workers. That influence may be subtle, but it's real. Put yourself in your workers' place. How could you feel going from a clean, neat home to a cluttered, littered plant? How unkempt would the workplace have to be to dampen your enthusiasm?

What about dirt that has been there so long it's noticed only by visitors. What kind of performance could you give under such conditions? If you had a chance to work in a bright and clean as opposed to dank and dirty place, which would you choose?

You know the answer. Improving the work environment may not seem to make that much difference in the short run, but in the long run it certainly will. And it presents a great opportunity for the new or renewed manager. It's a golden chance to do something beneficial and progressive without getting too many people angry about it.

Take the old and decrepit and make it shine. Cleaning and painting will work miracles. Give it a look that will make believers out of even the most skeptical. Turn the clutter into order and the dinginess into sparkle. The opportunity is ready made.

Clean and paint

Sure, you say, nothing to it. Except where's the money coming from? Who is going to finance this cleaning and painting extravaganza? You're on a tight financial string and the money's just not there. Maybe so, but you don't have to do everything at once. You can start on a small and limited budget and work wonders. If you want to do it, you can find a way.

Start with high-traffic areas—restrooms, for example. If your people don't take care of the restrooms, clean them up. Flat down scrub them clean. While you're cleaning, make sure they're all working and flushing and doing what they're supposed to. Don't say you can't get money to fix the plumbing. If it's true, you're in the wrong outfit. Then make sure they stay clean and in good working order. Even if you have to plunge a few yourself in the evening, keep them working. Don't shake your head; that is too one of the things you were hired for.

From the restrooms go to the break area. First, give it the old cleaneroo, including vending machines and floors. Get some fresh trash cans. Have people clean off the tables as they leave. Make sure the floors get mopped. If there are windows, finagle some curtains; they don't have to be fancy, just pleasant and bright. Make sure the tables and chairs are sturdy. If they're old, some paint will dress them up in a hurry.

If you can't paint much, pick some spots. Is there a particularly barren or severe area that would benefit from a splash of color? Hit that first. Look at the entrance. Is it pleasant? If not, start by painting the door jamb.

If you don't have any paint, beg some. That's right, beg some. That's part of what community relations are all about. Besides being a good guy, maybe you can get something for the plant once in a while. You're not trying to get enough to paint the entire building. There's no telling who is throwing away paint you can use. You don't even have to be particular. Battleship gray or pea green can be effective if used properly.

Follow the same process on out into the plant. Don't try for the whole banana at first. You'll need a little time to decide what you want to do. Start by accenting isolated areas. Like doors, window frames, or posts in the middle of the floor. Or awful-looking boxes and storage things.

If you have a choice, use a color that's outrageous. Find a bright, ungodly shade and splash it around. Orange is great. Yes, orange. Or bright yellow. Or chartreuse. Colors you wouldn't think of? Nonsense. Use them in areas that aren't connected and you'll be amazed at the transformation in your plant.

Don't worry about matching or making everything symmetrical, as long as your bright spots are removed from each other. And don't worry about pattern; there's no need. The tie-in will come when you paint the walls. The only caution here is to keep them light. Deeper colors can look pretty on the chart, but they get overpowering and depressing on walls. Light beige, light green, pale yellow, pastel blue are good basic colors to work with. They'll not only brighten the plant but will tie in the bright splashes and not fight them.

Don't worry about the old saw that says light-colored walls get dirty so much faster and need painting that much quicker. They really don't get bad that fast. You might have to watch and keep certain spots touched up, but by and large it's no problem. Besides, your place probably should be painted more often anyway.

And don't let your pocketbook be the only factor in determining the quality of paint you use. You'll hurt yourself and will have to repaint more often if you take the cheap way out. Shop around, talk to various dealers, and get the best grade for your money.

Keep it that way

When you get your place clean and painted, keep it that way. Don't let junk piles build up again, with conditions slowly deteriorating. Guard against the day-to-day accumulation of unsightly storage or waste. Don't let it creep up on you until suddenly you're back where you were.

Have the eyes of a stranger! Don't accept what you should be challenging.

Every time you have a chance, visit somebody else's plant. If it is well managed, so much the better. If it is poorly managed, you can profit from that too. Don't go to find fault. See what you can learn about the way your plant is and should be by comparing it with others, good and bad.

Sure, it's still a factory. And there are certain conditions that you'll have to live with. It won't be spotless everywhere, every day, all the time. But you can make the physical surroundings lighter and more cheerful. Determination will do wonders in making it a more habitable place.

Minor repairs can also make a difference. Make sure you replace burned-out light bulbs immediately. Keep restrooms, water fountains, and vending machines clean and in working order. Pay attention to small annoyances.

You say you've no one to look after that stuff? Your staff is limited and so is their time? It's going to be tough to cover it all? Yes, it would be if you weren't constantly on the alert—in the morning when you're out greeting, during your rounds, after everyone's gone home. Spot whatever needs to be fixed and get it done.

And while you're getting your plant physically the way you want it, think about getting it mentally the way you want it. Start with yourself. Don't be a sourpuss. You don't have to be a personality kid to smile occasionally. Encourage your supervisors to spread a smile or two around the place. If possible, have some music playing in the background off and on during the day. Brighten the atmosphere any way you can.

It will pay dividends! Your people will be more relaxed and more alert. They'll do better work. Production will be higher and quality will improve. People will want to be at work when they can, so absenteeism will drop. They'll talk about you favorably, so applicants will be higher.

You'll be able to generate the feeling that your plant is on the move. Employees will feel that they're a part of that movement and will be more willing to go where you lead them. Create the environment that will give you that return.

11 | DO WHAT YOU CAN

Even before you became manager there were lots of things you wanted to change. You started planning before you knew you were getting the job.

It started back when you began thinking you could do it better than the person in the job. Then, after you took over, it didn't take you long to see how the plant, and possibly the company, could use a real overhaul. You couldn't say so out loud, of course, but you secretly wondered how the place had survived for so long. There was no question in your mind that remedies were in order. What's more, you were certain you had some of those remedies, if only you had the authority.

But, let's face, you don't have it. Your authority is limited. It's frustrating! You have all these wonderful ideas that can't be put to use. First of all, stop worrying. Don't waste your time and energy over things you cannot change. Stewing over something you can do nothing about is the path to Ulcersville.

That doesn't mean you shouldn't be concerned about problems you see, whether they're within your purview or not. Keep in mind that your perspective may be limited; there may be considerations you are unfamiliar with. Even so, it's your duty to spot potential problems and to bring them to the attention of the powers-that-be. And if you feel strongly about something but are prohibited from doing it, talk to your boss. You've nothing to lose.

Don't be bashful about advocating changes that have merit. You don't have to be 100 percent right, as long as you've thought it out thoroughly. If it's a policy or procedure that has been around for a while, question why it was implemented in the first place. Check the background before recommending a dramatic change. There's no sense stepping on toes until you know whose toes. Why create turmoil and possible animosity blindly?

Once you're convinced, it's your duty to say something. Your chances of success will probably be greater if you tackle problems within the plant. But if you want to take a flyer on something companywide, do it if you're really sure. Bring it out in the open.

Then comes rejection! What then?

Accentuate the positive

Accept it, live with it! That's the way it is. Don't bang your head against the wall. Don't drag out the crying towel and bemoan the devastation the company will face from not adopting what you've offered.

That's self-defeating. You're wasting energy that you can put to better use changing the things you can. That's where you need to concentrate! There are so many things you can control, so many things that need to be done. A never-ending parade of opportunities falls within your authority. You just don't have the time to worry about what cannot be. It's pointless and unrewarding.

So accentuate the positive. Use your time and resources to plan the changes and improvements you can
control. Accept the challenge of what you have. If you
do that the way you should, you'll get the chance to do
more.

12 | FUN TIME

You can look at it in two ways. It's either a
tremendous pain in the tail or the exciting challenge
you live for.

What is it? Why, the impossible task that you'll be
asked to do from time to time. It's going to happen.
Sometime, somehow, somewhere, some of those salespeople are going to promise that you'll deliver what they
have no right to promise. It won't be logical or reasonable. You'll wonder how you could even consider such a
possibility, let alone promise it. Then you'll go ahead
and bust your back to do it!

Yes against all reason. When there is not even a hope
of doing it, when you know you're the one who will get
the short end of the stick, when you're convinced it's
unrealistic even to ask, you're going to do it. You may
not always know why. You may even think you're irra-
tional to attempt it. You realize there's a danger that if
you do it once you'll be expected to do it again, and
possibly again.

You'll take on the odds even though you know that it
wasn't you who created the predicament in the first
place. Sometimes it won't be anybody's fault. Other
times you'll know where the screw-up came from—it

was somebody in your own organization—but you won't be able to help yourself. You'll try to do the impossible anyway.

Now you'll be tempted not to do it. After all, the request is completely unrealistic and you can't be blamed if you can't. Why should you have to go through agony because of someone else? And you'll wonder if it's really all that necessary. Maybe it would be better in the long run if you didn't pull the jerks out of the jam. That would force them to do it right the next time. Could be, could be.

These are valid considerations. And certainly if it becomes an everyday occurrence, you have to put a stop to it. You cannot do it every day, no matter how good you are. Nobody can survive a steady crash diet.

True production success requires careful planning and a smooth operation. Even if your business calls for constant changes, you plan and program for them. You handle those changes smoothly because you're flexible in your thinking and train people for it.

Unplanned demands and changes upset the system. You can react to them in the short term. You can look great for a while, even kid yourself that it's easy. A little pushing, pulling, nothing to it. You're right, except it will eventually catch up with you. You can live from crisis to crisis for only so long. Most people are not equipped to operate that way for any length of time. You cannot accept one impossible task after another without crippling your normal operation.

That's when you must seriously question your superiors as to the advisability of continuing harem-scarem. You must ask if it is really necessary. Don't worry about being called a quitter or traitor or any of those nasty things. Your responsibility is to produce the most and the best, and when outside factors will not let you it's up to you to scream.

Life blood

But the occasional exception is different. Sometimes there is no escaping the fact that the impossible would be best for the company. You understand the reasons and agree that it should be done. The only fact you have to deal with is that it's there to do. And it's up to you to do it. Can you?

Yes! Because that's when it all comes together, that's when the adrenalin starts to flow. It may not be the moment you live for, but it sure adds spice to your everyday life. It's you and no one else against the world. It's you defying and conquering reason. It's you with a shot at the impossible dream.

You should thrive on it! Welcome it as that new challenge, as that rare opportunity when you can really enjoy being a manager. Because that's when managing's fun! Day-to-day managing is important—it's the meat and potatoes—but it's not one continuous thrill. The good manager gets the job done with a minimum of flash and fanfare. The kicks come not from high rolling but from the satisfaction of a quiet, routine performance that gets results. The successful manager is patient and is willing to go back to the same problem again and again until it's right—and willing to go back once more if it happens again.

One of your goals should be to take the excitement out of the job. If it's too exciting there's something wrong. Sure there should be some, but you're working for the calm, which is gratifying and productive. On that basis, welcome the impossible. Use it to see what kind of manager you really are. See if you've listened to your own preaching and if you've prepared your people properly.

When you're asked to perform it, first decide if it is really an impossible task or just seems like one. You are the best judge. It is possible that it is impossible. If so, make the decision and tell everyone concerned. Stick to your guns if you're absolutely sure. Don't tell your people you can do it just because that's what they want to hear. You'll be doing them a great disservice. It's better to tell the truth and face a temporary setback than have them count on what you cannot do and fail.

But more than likely the task isn't impossible. Remember, tough is not the same as impossible. Pushed to the last extremity is not the same as impossible. Above and beyond is not the same as impossible. So while you're figuring if it can be done, figure out how it would go if it could. Figure out who has to be involved, who has to get it done. Think through what extra effort is required.

Let them do it

Then when you go, make sure all your people know about it. Make sure they know exactly what the job is, why it's important, how each participant fits into the scheme of things. Make sure they know who else is involved and what time frame they are going to have to work in. Communicate—the magic word—to everyone. Make sure all the moves are coordinated.

Then step back and let your people do it. It's their ballgame now. Naturally you have to monitor to keep the project on schedule. If it's not, find out why; if outside help is needed, supply it. But stay out of the way. If the situation changes, you must make sure everyone knows. You're the umpire, and if the rules change, the players should know.

They've got to know. They are the producers, the ones who determine if you meet the challenge successfully or not. Let's face it, your workers are the people who will really be going above and beyond. And that's as it should be. Your thrill will come from seeing those you've worked so hard with come through in the crunch. When your people react positively because of your time and effort, it's your triumph.

So educate, motivate, coordinate, and calculate; but let them be the ones who do. And when they've done it, let them know what they've done. Let them know that everyone knows they've done it. Thank them, praise them, recognize them. Then give yourself a little pat on the back. They did the job, but you made it possible. That's where your satisfaction should come from.

Getting the impossible done through others is a great feeling. Enjoy it. If you're that good, you won't have much time to savor it.

13 | INNOVATE

One remarkable thing about inexperienced plant managers: they'll try things more experienced and smarter managers won't. Because the newer ones don't know any better.

The older and wiser manager knows all those new ideas won't work; there's no use even trying. So the old-timer just plows ahead, secure in the knowledge that there's no reason to do anything differently.

Then comes the young, happy, new manager who doesn't know any better. The dumbbell presses ahead with some project, not understanding that it's impossible, that it's been tried before and discarded or thought about but not tried.

So what happens? It works! The manager thought it

could work and proceeded on that basis. And lo and behold, it worked! It worked in spite of the odds against introducing something new and complicated and foreign. It worked even when those with experience said it was impossible. Success came because the young manager thought it would work and did it.

It can be done

There are a few who will accomplish what the many will not, because the few believe it can be done while the many believe it cannot be done. This is not an oversimplification. Many of the greatest managerial breakthroughs come through the efforts of those who aren't experienced enough to know that it isn't possible.

It happens frequently when a manager moves from one discipline to another. What is normal in one industry or company has never been tried in another. Often it's been considered, but for some reason it's never been tried. Then along comes a new manager who knows it will work, is used to having it work, and plunges straight ahead. The results are fantastic, because of the knowledge that they will be.

The deciding factor is not so much the task itself as the attitude of the individual attempting the task. The manager who believes it can be done will do it. The one who believes it cannot be done will be absolutely correct.

Be determined

A word of caution. It's not enough just to believe something can be done. That's only the starting point. Second, and equally important, is the determination to succeed. You must make up your mind that whatever you're about to introduce will work. You will have to be bullheaded in your purpose, especially if it's a major or radical change.

Of course, you can't be fanatical—your workers may accuse you of this anyway—because you may encounter unknown factors. The situation may not develop exactly as you envisioned. You may have missed something along the road. If so, don't be stupid. You've no choice but to come off it. Just don't be premature. Before abandoning a good idea, look to see if some modification will make a difference. Maybe a minor move here or there will do it.

Or it could be your people dragging their feet, being stubborn, actually stooping to sabotage. It's not impossible. Don't be put off by normal resistance. Expect it and overcome it.

Often normal resistance stops the experienced manager from even trying. It's happened to many. It's not that they can't think of new ideas. It's not that they don't see things that should be changed. And it's not that they don't realize things could be better.

The stopper is that they think it won't work because people will resist. So they're reluctant to try. What they don't understand is that their reluctance is based on a history of tentative trying, or resistance more apparent than real, or no persistence in execution, or lack of true commitment.

That's where the new and ignorant have the great advantage. All they know is that it will work. They're not haunted by the specter of past failures. They're convinced that all they have to do is educate people, put it into effect, and make sure it's done. What's simple for them is impossible for others. As a result they succeed where others fail. It all comes back to believing it can be done.

Do it

Be a believer. Sure there are problems, but you cannot let them stop you from trying—and doing. When you start out you'll see literally hundreds of things that could be better. But you cannot rush in pell-mell and make changes. You must first analyze, plan, and evaluate. Then move into the preparation stage. Get the information for the final decisions. If you think you should go, go!

Initially your people will be slow to react. It will take a lot of prodding. There is no such thing as a small change to the people who have to do it. Even when they've been through one and know how it's helped, they'll resist the next. So you'll need the same thorough preparation, indoctrination, implementation, and follow-up on the last change as on the first. It's human nature and you can't get around that.

A complete change, large or small, is a complex undertaking. The thorough preparation and the past successes are only underpinnings for the future. They're the foundation you build on, the foundation you must use every time out of the chute.

And you're going to be coming out of that chute many times, because it's a sure bet that plenty of changes need to be made. One of your greatest challenges as a manager will be to introduce those changes that are necessary and practical. It's up to you to try things that have never been tried before—or retry things that should have worked but for some reason didn't.

But guard against changing for the sake of changing. There are so many more important things to do. Don't make changes just to suit your way of doing things, especially at first; you can ease into them when your people get used to you. But if a change will not make any difference in the operation, why stir everyone up? You're liable to do more harm than good.

There'll be plenty of real needs. You won't be able to count the opportunities for the quantum jump. When they come, take the chance! Be ignorant of that thing called failure. Dare to innovate—and prosper.